COUNTRY

ROADS OF

Alabama

D1607486

COUNTRY ROADS OF

Alabama

Carol Thalimer
with Dan Thalimer

ILLUSTRATED BY CLIFF WINNER

COUNTRY ROADS PRESS
OAKS, PENNSYLVANIA

Country Roads of Alabama

Published by Country Roads Press
P.O. Box 838, 2170 West Drive
Oaks, PA 19456

Text design by Richard Heinberg.
Cover Illustration © 1996 by Michael McCurdy.
Illustrations by Cliff Winner.
Typesetting by Allen Crider

ISBN 1-56626-131-7

Library of Congress Cataloging-in-Publication Data
Thalimer, Carol.
    Country roads of Alabama / author, Carol Thalimer: illustra-
tor, Cliff Winner.
        p.   cm.
    Includes index.
    ISBN 1-56626-131-7
    1. Alabama—Guidebooks. 2. Automobile travel—Alabama—
Guidebooks. I. Thalimer, Dan. II. Title.
F324.3.T43 1995
917.6104'63—dc20   95-10223
                                                                    CIP

Printed in Canada.
10 9 8 7 6 5 4 3 2 1

To all the Alabama relatives past and present—especially
Marie Davis and the late William E. Davis

CONTENTS

ACKNOWLEDGMENTS

The friendly folks in Alabama obviously love their state, and their enthusiasm rubs off on others. In addition to the immense assistance we received from traveling companions *extraordinaire* Heather Roberts Rickles and Dixie Martino, both formerly of the State of Alabama Bureau of Tourism and Travel, dozens of other people helped us with our research and took countless hours to show us around. Just a few of them are Lisa Greer, also formerly of the Bureau, Jennifer Carr and Kelly Burt of the Montgomery Convention and Visitors Bureau (CVB), Sherry Vallides of Southern Tours in Marion, Kristin Odom of the Tuscaloosa Convention and Visitors Bureau, Richard Kinne of the Black Belt Tourism Association, Pat Dakin of the Auburn/Opelika CVB, Ralph Stacy of the Greenville Area Chamber of Commerce, Sandy Smith of the Monroeville Chamber of Commerce/CVB, Cindy Bailey of the Calhoun County Chamber of Commerce, Lloyd Waggon of the Gadsden/Etowah County Tourism Association, Edie Jones of the Selma/Dallas County Chamber of Commerce, Jerry Paasch of the Decatur CVB, Donald Dorr of the Bayou La Batre/Coden Tourism Commission, and Jack Jones, who represented Mentone. We'd also like to thank the dozens of hospitable Alabamians who fed us or put us up while we explored the state.

INTRODUCTION

In 1849 my great-great-great-grandfather, Vincent Bell, and six of his eleven sons migrated to Lowndes County in central Alabama from Camden, South Carolina, to take advantage of the first open land south of Montgomery. Family marriages, births, and deaths are recorded in Hayneville, Mt. Willing, Calhoun, Letohatchee, and Fort Deposit. The men in the family attended the University of Alabama, and the women attended Judson College in Marion. My uncle, Joseph Bell, attended the Marion Military Institute in Marion before being appointed to West Point.

The stately Victorian home of my great-grandparents—Vincent Hardy Bell and Lula Cheek Garrett Bell—still stands amid extensive lawns at the junction of US 185 and Bell Street in Fort Deposit. I remember visiting it as a child and thinking it was the grandest house I'd ever seen. Even from an adult's point of view, it is still a wonderful house.

Although I lived in Alabama only a short time while my father was stationed at what was then Camp Rucker, I'm now right next door in Georgia, so I have many opportunities to explore my heritage and enjoy the highways and byways of Alabama—a fascinating state where grand antebellum mansions laze in the sun near a 354-foot Saturn V rocket; where the birthplace of the modern Civil Rights Movement exists on the very site of the Cradle of the Confederacy; where an abandoned steel mill evolved into a community center.

A large and topographically diverse state, Alabama stretches 330 miles from the Gulf Coast to the Appalachian Mountains. Elevation varies from sea level to 2,407 feet at Cheaha State Park. The state's thirty-three million acres include almost one million acres of inland water, and Alabama boasts one of the most extensive river systems in the country. Two-thirds of the state is covered in forest. Alabama is the only place in the world where you can find all three components for making steel—coal, iron ore, and limestone—within a ten-mile radius.

We've heard some priceless sayings about the state's varied topography, such as, "Alabama's the only place where you can stand knee-deep in mud and still get dust in your eye," and "Alabama's the only state where you can find a swamp on top of a mountain."

Archeological excavations reveal that man has lived in Alabama since 10,000 B.C. The Choctaw Indians were among the first residents in modern history. The name Alabama came from the Albaamo Indians, a farming tribe. *Alba* meant dense or mass vegetation, and *amo* meant to clear; thus the name *Albaamo* denoted "thicket clearers." The Spanish were the first whites to explore Alabama. Although they arrived in 1519 and 1528, it was the Hernando de Soto expedition in 1540 that fully explored the region. The French founded Mobile in 1702 but lost out to the British in 1763. Alabama entered the Union in 1819.

The term "Dixie" originally evolved in Alabama, where the French issued ten-dollar notes that carried the French word *dix* meaning "ten." Eventually the South became Dixie Land.

Although Decatur, Selma, and Tuscaloosa were heavily damaged during the Civil War, Alabama was fortunate to escape the devastation that other southern states such as Georgia experienced. As a result, the state boasts scores of antebellum homes, many of which are open to tour.

Travelers craving the Old South can follow their fancy back in time through the device of a pilgrimage. The very word evokes hoop-skirts, parasols, and soft drawls. These journeys into the South's stately homes were actually initiated by impoverished ladies trying to raise money to save their homes after the Civil War.

Pilgrimages are offered in Alabama almost year round. Spring pilgrimages are highlighted by flamboyant floral beauty. Christmas tours are often given by candlelight. Sample the pilgrimages in Athens, Cullman, Eufaula, Eutaw, Huntsville, Mobile, Monroeville, Montgomery, Mooresville, Opelika, Prattville, Selma, Talladega, Tuscaloosa, and Union Springs. Several other communities sponsor pilgrimages every other year.

The South as a region has more museums than any other area in the nation, and Alabama is no exception to that fact. Pride in heritage runs deep. A standard feature in practically every town, village, or crossroads is a local history or house museum.

Above and beyond the lure of Alabama's natural landmarks and fascinating historic attractions is the state's famed southern hospitality. Because of my family connections, I'm always welcomed into the bosom of every community, but complete strangers to the state are treated as honored guests as well.

Alabama's friendliness is often ascribed to a thirst for commonality: "We'll ask you questions 'til we find somebody we both know," explains Ralph Stacy of the Greenville Chamber of Commerce. "Then we'll have lots to talk about."

Take this guide to Alabama (which we've arranged in convenient trip routes), get a good highway map, and explore the Heart of Dixie. The routes we've chosen cover a fairly manageable area, so that you can explore them in as little as a long weekend. However, allot more time than you think you'll need; you'll almost surely ferret out other little gems and spend endless hours making new friends along the way.

The Black Belt Trail crosses a geographic region in west central Alabama that stretches 228 miles from Eutaw to Camden. The Chattahoochee Trace runs 487 miles north to south with sidetrips along the Alabama/Georgia border from Lafayette to the Florida border. The Road to Civil Rights in central Alabama begins in Selma and traverses 300 miles to Tuskegee. The Coastal Circle Trail covers 155 miles circling Mobile Bay and includes the Gulf Coast beaches. The Lookout Mountain Parkway stretches 101 miles with side trips from the Alabama/Georgia/Tennessee border to Gadsden. On the Trail of Lost Luggage runs 152 miles through northeast Alabama from Oxford/Anniston to Albertville. Bridging the Gaps explores 212 miles of off-the-beaten-track areas in northwest Alabama. The Swinging South Trail begins in Tallassee and runs 261 miles south to the Monroeville area. The Tennessee River Heritage Trail follows the river 197 miles from the Alabama/Mississippi border in extreme northwest Alabama to the Alabama/Georgia/Tennessee border in the extreme northeastern corner of the state. Fields of Greens explores the 342-mile Robert Trent Jones Golf Trail.

For the most part, we've concentrated on historical attractions and natural landmarks, rather than on amusement parks, recreational activities, or shopping. We do not include days and hours of operation or admission prices, because they are all so changeable. Particularly in very small towns, museums and such may only be open a few days a month or by appointment. Some attractions of major architectural and/or historical significance are private homes that are not open to the public or are open only for special occasions such as pilgrimages or historic home tours; thus you may only be able to walk or drive by.

Every effort has been made to supply current and correct information, but things do change or even close. For the most up-to-date details on any of the places we've described, check with the local welcome center or local tourist organization when you plan your trip or when you get to the area.

Alabama is such a large and fascinating state that we've still left several areas and significant towns untouched. Get in your car and create your own trail for a memorable vacation.

CHAPTER 1

THE BLACK BELT TRAIL

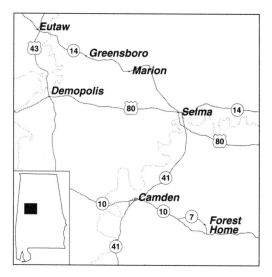

slender band of rolling prairie underlaid with rich black soil runs between the northern and southern regions of the Gulf Coastal Plain. Known as the Black Belt, it was perfect for growing cotton in the early to mid 1800s. The Alabama, Tombigbee, Cahaba, Coosa, Tallapoosa, and Black Warrior Rivers created waterborne highways that enabled the cotton to be shipped all over the world. Steamboat landings, some with long chutes from the cliffs above, lined the riverbanks. The area was soon so wealthy with profits from King Cotton that opulent plantation homes dotted the landscape.

A significant amount of cotton is still grown in the Black Belt, but the area now supports major cattle and soybeans industries as well. Timber farming, especially on the marginal acreage, is restoring the natural beauty of the area's woodlands. In addition to the magnificent antebellum mansions and other historic sites, wildlife and natural attractions entice thousands of visitors to the Black Belt each year.

The towns of the Black Belt include Camden, Demopolis, Eutaw, Greensboro, Marion, and Selma. We begin our 228-mile exploration of the Black Belt in **Marion.** Located on State 14 northwest of Selma, Marion is the home of Judson College and the Marion Military Institute. The gracious town has an illustrious past as a cultural and educational center. At one time the small town boasted five institutions of higher learning. In addition to the two surviving schools, the town was home to the Marion Female Seminary, Howard College (now Samford University in Birmingham), and Lincoln Normal School for freed slaves. Alabama State University, now in Montgomery, also began in Marion.

Spared destruction during the Civil War, the Marion you see today is what you envision when you imagine the serenity, elegance, and beauty of the Old South. This gem of a town boasts a hundred and seventy-five antebellum homes, churches, and other historic structures.

Judson College, founded in 1838, is one of the oldest women's colleges in the United States and the only one in Alabama. The Alabama Women's Hall of Fame, located on the campus in A. Howard Bean Hall (334-683-5242), honors such women as Helen Keller, Lurleen Wallace, Julia Strudwick Tutwiler, Amelia Gayle Gorgas, Tallulah Bankhead, and Mildred Westervelt Warner. Bronze plaques, portraits, letters, and other memorabilia describe their contributions to Alabama. Built of pressed brick, the structure is elegantly embellished with Ionic columns and cornices painted white to resemble the marble porticoes of classical Greece. Inside, the woodwork and furniture are of Old Mission style.

Marion Military Institute was founded in 1842 as the Baptist Manual Labor School; then it became Howard College and was renamed Samford University when it moved to Birmingham. The school eventually became a military preparatory school and junior college (1101 South Washington Street, 334-683-2343 or 800-448-4084). Eighty-five percent of its graduates go on to one of the U.S. service academies.

The school's lovely chapel, built in 1857, served as a Confederate hospital during the Civil War. Countless names and initials of former students and patients are carved into the handmade brick exterior walls. Several lovely stained-glass windows were acquired in the early 1900s: the University of Pennsylvania Window, the University of Virginia Window, the Woodrow Wilson Window, the Aristotle Window, the Milton Window, and the Princeton Window.

Also on the campus is the Alabama Military Hall of Honor, where portrait plaques of inductees are displayed along with military artifacts. This charming building has had a long and diverse history. It was constructed in 1832 to house a law office; later it became the meeting place of the Young Men's Christian Association; then the local chapter of the United Daughters of the Confederacy was organized there in 1903. Finally, it served as Marion's City Hall from 1928 to 1968, before it was moved to the grounds of the military school in 1988.

An Episcopal church was established in Marion in 1838, the same year in which Judson College was founded. A parish school was established in 1849, and the name "St. Wilfrid's" was taken for both the church and the school (104 Clement Street, 334-683-6562). Walter C. Whitaker wrote in his 1898 book *The Church in Alabama*: "The times were especially propitious for such schools, as no scheme of common-school education at public expense had yet been broached, and the schools were long in a flourishing condition in many places, notably in Mobile, Montgomery, Tuskaloosa [sic], and Marion. In the last named place the Rev. W.A. Stickney's school was especially successful, numbering more than 80 pupils and having a standing list of applicants for vacancies year after year." His words are just another affirmation that tiny Marion was as progressive in matters of education as Alabama's larger cities.

Since St. Wilfrid's founding there have been several church buildings on the site, because the previous ones were victims of fires. The present structure was built in 1908, but the cemetery goes back to 1849. Civil War soldiers from both the Confederacy and the Union who died while hospitalized at the Marion Military Institute were originally buried there. In 1872, the Ladies' Memorial Association of Marion was formed. They moved the Civil War dead to a section of St. Wilfrid's cemetery and marked all the graves. About half are known and the other half unknown. The most prominent person buried there is William Brooks, the Perry County native who served as the president of the Alabama Secession Convention in January 1861. Numerous family plots have graves where the birth dates go back as far as the late 1700s. Another section of the cemetery was reserved for the bodies of slaves of parishioners.

One of Marion's most renowned teachers was Nicola Marschall, a Prussian portrait painter who settled in Marion to teach art and music. Marschall designed the Stars and Bars of the Confederacy, which was then stitched by several local ladies. He also designed the grey Confederate uniforms and painted portraits of both Confederate and Union leaders, many of whom were his friends. Among his best-known portraits are Generals Robert E. Lee, Nathan Bedford Forrest, U.S. Vice President John C. Breckenridge, Confederate President Jefferson Davis, and Presidents Ulysses S. Grant and Abraham Lincoln. Marschall's own self-portrait hangs in the First White House of the Confederacy in Montgomery.

Marion has many homes you should drive by. In 1840, Texas hero Sam Houston married Margaret Lea in a small 1830 raised cottage now known as the Lea-Kramer Home on West Greene Street. The home of Secession Governor Andrew Barry Moore and a home used as a headquarters by Confederate General Nathan Bedford Forrest are only a few of Marion's historic sites.

Other significant structures include the 1830s Cocke-Gibler Home and the 1859 Peters Home, both noted for their intricate saw work; and Greek Revival homes such as Reverie, built in 1850, and the Caffee-Lovelace Home, built in 1860. Another Greek Revival home, the 1849 Camellia Place, is an antique shop. Carlisle Hall, built in 1857, is an outstanding example of Italianate architecture. Each spring Marion sponsors a pilgrimage featuring tours of many of the historic homes, an antique show and sale, and other activities. Homes are also open for a Christmas tour in December.

Marion has several illustrious black residents. Coretta Scott King, widow of Martin Luther King Jr., and Jean Young, the late wife of Andrew Young, were from Marion. They met when Young was the pastor of a Marion church.

Visit the monument to Harry The Slave in the Marion Cemetery. In 1854, 23-year-old Harry was employed as a janitor at Howard College. When a fire broke out in the middle of the night, he lost his life while waking everyone. Due to his actions, only one student died. Harry was honored with a funeral attended by nearly everyone in Marion, then buried in the main part of the cemetery rather than in the slave section. His bravery is memorialized on a large monument erected by the students of the college and the Alabama Baptist Convention.

Antique hunters find rich feeding ground in Marion. Ten dealers located in historic homes or turn-of-the-century shops have banded together to form the Marion Antique Dealers Association (103 Jefferson Street, 334-683-2004).

Accommodations are available in several antebellum homes. Myrtle Hill (303-305 West Lafayette Street, 334-683-9095) was the 1840 Greek Revival home of George D. Johnson, a brigadier general for the Confederate States of America. Before the Civil War he served as the mayor of Marion and in the Alabama Legislature. After the war he was the Commandant of Cadets at the University of Alabama, then superintendent of the South Carolina Military Academy (The Citadel), and, finally, an Alabama senator.

Lovingly restored by Wanda and Gerald Lewis and elegantly furnished with eighteenth- and nineteenth-century antiques, Myrtle Hill offers spacious accommodations. Enjoy a sumptuous plantation breakfast in the formal dining room, and be sure to ask about the ghost.

Sherry Vallides, owner of Southern Tours, offers elegant bed-and-breakfast accommodations at Reverie (West Lafayette Street, 334-683-6100), her stunning 1850s Greek Revival mansion. Sherry is the best source in town for anything you want to know about Marion and Perry County.

Built in the early 1800s, Myatt-Drew-Duck Bed and Breakfast (304 West Greene Street, 334-683-6309) is the only house in town that features identical pedimented porticoes in both the front and back of the house. Three exquisitely furnished bed-and-breakfast rooms are offered.

For a substantial lunch or dinner, the most popular place in town is The Gateway Inn Dinner Club overlooking the golf course (1615 State 5 South, 334-683-9166). The dining hall at Judson College is open to the public, and meals there are economically priced.

Take State 14 west to **Greensboro.** As one of Alabama's best-preserved antebellum communities, Greensboro contains more than 150 historic structures ranging in style from mansions to cottages to commercial buildings. Magnolia Grove (1002 Hobson Street, 334-624-8618) is an 1840 temple-form Greek Revival mansion built by Colonel Isaac Croom. It was the birthplace of his grand-nephew Rear Admiral Richmond Pearson Hobson, hero of the Spanish-American War.

The interior—a work in progress—is furnished with antiques that belonged to either the Hobson or Croom families. Landscaped with traditional garden plants of the Old South, the twelve-acre site includes a detached kitchen building, a servant's cottage, and a building that served as a library-office or classroom.

The Noel-Ramsey House, sometimes called The Old French House, (Market and South Streets, 334-624-8344), was constructed between 1819 and 1821 by Thomas Noel. It is the only surviving residence built by settlers of the Vine and Olive Colony, which comprised a group of exiles from Napoleon's army who emigrated to America to grow grapes for wine and olives. Most of them settled around Demopolis, so you'll hear more about the colony when we describe that city.

Although Noel was part of the colony, he had spent some time in the West Indies before coming to Greensboro. This Caribbean influence is evident in the architecture of the house. A hipped roof flares over the recessed double-tiered gallery, and the porch is supported by slim, wooden Tuscan colonnettes.

A side hall (uncommon in West Alabama), double flanking rooms on the first floor, and a hall and single dormitory room on the second floor characterized the original house plan. Additions modified the house over the years.

The house remained in the family until the 1980s, when it was deeded to the Hale County Preservation Society. Today, it is filled with original and period furnishings and a wealth of family memorabilia.

Blue Shadows Guest House (State 14 west, 334-624-3637), a country bed and breakfast on three hundred and twenty acres, offers elegant accommodations, a formal garden, nature trails, a pond, and a bird sanctuary.

Stay on State 14 west to the northern end of the Black Belt at **Eutaw,** the county seat of Greene County. The county is named for Revolutionary War hero Nathanael Greene, and the town is named for his most significant victory against the British, the Battle of Eutaw Springs, South Carolina.

Hundreds of years ago this area—already the home of the well-established Choctaw and Chickasaw Indian nations—was visited by De Soto in 1540 and by Jean Baptiste Le Moyne, Sieur de Bienville in 1736. In the early 1800s, several communities of pioneer farmers and herdsmen sprang up along the Sipsey, Warrior, and Tombigbee Rivers—a region found to be ideal for growing cotton. Mesopotamia, which means "a high place between two waters," was founded in the early 1800s, and Old Springfield was founded in 1818. When Eutaw was founded in 1838 it absorbed both towns.

The Tombigbee and Warrior Rivers became lifelines for the communities along their banks and bluffs. During the Golden Era from 1840 to 1860, Eutaw prospered from cotton. The crop was loaded onto steamboats bound for Mobile, and return boats brought supplies, dry goods, and extravagances for the opulent planters' lifestyles.

Fifty-three town homes and mansions survive from that era, because after the Union army burned Tuscaloosa, they marched on to Mississippi, sparing Eutaw and the surrounding communities. The antebellum homes, combined with dozens more from the Victorian period, make Eutaw a popular tourist attraction. Get the brochure entitled "A Walking and Driving Guide" from the Greene County Visitor Center, located in the historic Vaughn-Morrow House (310 Main Street, 205-372-2871). The tour includes twenty-five historic homes and sites.

Kirkwood (111 Kirkwood Drive, 205-372-9009), the most-photographed house in Alabama, is open for tours. Just prior to the Civil War, Foster Mark Kirksey, a successful cotton merchant and factor, bought ninety-seven acres of land and began construction of a grand Greek Revival home while he was still a bachelor. The four-story mansion features eight gigantic Ionic columns and is crowned by a large belvedere or cupola. Kirksey shipped cotton to Europe and imported such luxuries for his home as eight Carrara-marble mantels from northern Italy and Waterford chandeliers from Ireland. Panes of different colored glass around the front door represent the four seasons. Kirksey married in 1860, when the house was almost complete, and he and his wife had the first of their seven children. However, construction came to an abrupt halt when the Civil War broke out in April 1861.

After the war the parlor was commandeered as a place where Southerners came to sign the oath of loyalty to the Union. Kirksey's fortunes were never regained, and the detail work on the mansion was never completed. Family members kept on living there until 1953, while the house continued on its downward spiral of deterioration. Then it sat abandoned for another ten years, its condition almost irreparable.

It was in 1972 that Mr. and Mrs. Roy Swayze first saw Kirkwood. So drawn were they to the house that they left their home in Virginia and began a ten-year odyssey to restore Kirkwood to its former splendor.

Kirkwood is a grand Greek Revival mansion with
eight long Ionic columns

They scoured the area for old materials such as slave-made bricks and heart-pine beams and flooring. They searched high and low for craftsmen who could do the intricate plaster cornice work. It took the experts one month per room to repair the ornamental moldings. The belvedere, which had been removed years before because of its unsafe condition, was restored and replaced. Mrs. Swayze says the project was "like putting a puzzle together." It took fourteen months to complete.

When the Swayzes decided to replace the wooden porch steps with stone, they located a supply of rejected Union tombstones. They found appropriate ironwork to complete the second-floor balcony that was never finished because of the Civil War. Then the hunt began for period furnishings and embellishments to complement the remaining original pieces. The third floor has been returned to its original purpose as a billiard room, and the Swayzes have added a small museum room packed with items they found on the property. In 1982, First Lady Nancy Reagan presented the Swayzes with the Honor Award from the National Trust for Historic Preservation for their outstanding restoration work.

Although Mr. Swayze has since died, Mrs. Swayze still conducts the tours and also offers elegant bed-and-breakfast accommodations.

Another bed and breakfast in Eutaw is the Humble House (401 Main Street, 205-372-9297), where owner Elizabeth Humble's twin daughters are the fifth generation of her family to live in the 1840 house, which is listed on the National Register of Historic Places. Spacious rooms, elegant furnishings, restful porches, and a delicious breakfast add to the charm.

If you can wrench yourself out of the nineteenth century, Eutaw also offers a modern diversion. Greenetrack, the Greene County Greyhound Park, Inc. (I-59 at Exit 45, 205-372-9318), presents racing you can watch from the comfort of the climate-controlled clubhouse.

From Eutaw take US 43/State 13 south to **Forkland,** where Jim Bird's sense of humor is expressed through his hay art. In the fields of his farm alongside County 69, Bird has used hay to create a giant locomotive, a hand holding a pair of scissors, animals, faces, and other flights of fancy.

Continue south on US 43/State 13 to **Demopolis.** In 1817, a band of exiles from Napoleon Bonaparte's army emigrated to the area, landing at the White Cliffs around what is now Demopolis to start the Vine and Olive Colony. These exiles were aristocrats who knew next to nothing about farming, and both the weather and the soil turned out to be inhospitable. Although their original plans for the colony failed, a new community was formed and given a name meaning "of the people, a city."

Perched on a high chalk cliff overlooking the Tombigbee River, Bluff Hall (407 North Commissioners Avenue, 334-289-1666) was built by slaves in 1832 as Allen Glover's wedding gift to his daughter. Named for the bluff on which it stands, the mansion represents two major trends in Southern architecture. The original house was a plain Federal-style townhouse. By 1850 the Greek Revival style had become more fashionable, and a columned front portico was added.

During the Civil War many Confederate officers—including Jefferson Davis and General Leonides Polk, the fighting preacher—were guests at Bluff Hall. Now a museum, the house is furnished with Empire and early Victorian pieces.

Even more impressive than the house itself and its furnishings is Bluff Hall's impressive display of antique clothing, which features more than five hundred pieces in a wide variety of styles, including a Mason's formal dress uniform; a baby dress that belonged to Israel Pickens, Alabama's first governor; wedding, christening, day, and party dresses; mourning clothes; nightgowns; and all kinds of accessories such as hats, gloves, fans, shawls, petticoats, corsets, and bloomers.

Bluff Hall's gift shop, located in a detached building that once served as an office, features handmade articles, historical pictures, books, and other gift items.

Gaineswood (805 South Cedar Avenue, 334-289-3220), a twenty-room Greek Revival mansion, took planter Nathan Whitfield more than seventeen years to complete. He named the estate for the Choctaw Indian agent around whose log cabin the mansion was created. *The Smithsonian Guide to Historic America: The Deep South* calls Gaineswood "one of the three or four most interesting houses in America—remarkable for its lavish Greek Revival interior and for the imposing arrangement of its porticoes and other architectural elements."

Galleried rooms filled with original furnishings are flooded with light from ceiling domes and accented with plaster friezes. An unusual feature is the generous use of interior cast-iron ornamentation. Whitfield was also an inventor who devised a musical instrument somewhat like a giant music box or one-man band which he called a flutina.

Considered the gateway to the 234-mile Tennessee-Tombigbee water system, modern Demopolis sports the new Demopolis Yacht Basin, which offers full service facilities for both pleasure and commercial boats.

In addition to recreational opportunities throughout the year, the river is the site of a spectacular week-long Christmas festival. The week kicks off with the naming of St. Nicholas. The honorary saint, who can be male or female, is chosen for contributions of time and talent to the community. St. Nicholas arrives by boat and is welcomed ashore at the City Landing by school children holding colorful lanterns they have made.

Activities include a musical show; performances by a living Christmas tree—a choir standing in the formation of a Christmas tree; candlelight tours of Bluff Hall, Gaineswood, and Foscue House; a children's street parade; and an arts and crafts festival. Civil War re-enactors camp out on the grounds of Gaineswood. Recently added to the roster of activities is a nationally sanctioned barbecue cook-off. Capping the week of the first Saturday in December is a spectacular boat parade during which Christmas scenes created with thousands of tiny light bulbs float down the river. The finale is a thrilling fireworks display.

From Demopolis take US 80 east to **Selma.** On the way you'll pass through Faunsdale, a small community that's experiencing a rebirth. Stop to eat at the Faunsdale Bar and Grill (US 80, 334-628-3240). Located behind an old storefront, the restaurant specializes in steaks and seafood and offers live entertainment on weekends. After you've investigated the important black heritage/civil rights attractions in Selma (see the Road to Civil Rights chapter), survey the rest of the charming city, which was laid out by William Rufus King, a vice-president of the United States who was named for one of Ossian's poems.

The jewel in Selma's crown is Sturdivant Hall, built in 1853 (713 Mabry Street, 334-872-5626). An outstanding example of neoclassical architecture, the ten-room mansion filled with period furniture is set amid formal gardens of flowers, trees, and shrubs. An exceptional museum gift shop is located in the original kitchen outbuilding.

Adjacent to Sturdivant Hall is Heritage Village (334-875-7241). Its five relocated historic structures include the McKinnon-Riggs doctor's office, which was used as a lawyer's office around 1852 and as a doctor's office around 1871; the 1830 Calhoun law office; the 1880s Siegel servant house; the 1830 Gillis House; and even a historic pigeon cote. On the other side of Sturdivant Hall is the 1858 White-Force Cottage (811 Mabry Street, 334-875-1714). Once the home of Martha Todd White, Mary Todd Lincoln's half-sister, it is now used for special functions.

Grace Hall (506 Lauderdale Street, 334-875-5744) is a bed-and-breakfast that is also open for public tours. The 1857 mansion is a consummate example of the delightful eclecticism that pervaded Alabama architecture after 1850. Renovations in 1870 and 1890 resulted in a gallery attached to the servant's quarters, a New Orleans-style courtyard with a central fountain, and a Williamsburg English garden and courtyard. The bed-and-breakfast rooms are located in the main house and in the servants' quarters. An overnight stay includes a tour of the house, full breakfast, morning coffee, and afternoon wine.

Two Selma districts you should visit are Historic Water Avenue and the Old Town Historic District. Water Avenue, which runs along the river, is a restored nineteenth-century commercial district with brick streets, antique stores, restaurants, fountains, and a restored bridge-tender's house. Several parks along the way are Bienville Park, Songs of Selma Park, and Lafayette Park. Both the National Voting Rights Museum and the Old Depot Museum (which in addition to its black heritage exhibits has an extensive collection of memorabilia relating to local history) are in this district. Enjoy lunch or dinner at Major Grumbles (1 Grumbles Alley, 334-872-2006), a restaurant overlooking the river.

The Old Town Historic District is one of the oldest residential districts in the state and includes Sturdivant Hall. A Windshield Tour brochure and audiotape, available at the Chamber of Commerce (513 Lauderdale Street, 334-875-7241 or 800-628-4291 in Alabama), describes a hundred and sixteen historic sites.

Confederate soldiers and prominent Selma citizens are immortalized on gravestones and statues in the Old Live Oak Cemetery (off US 22, 334-875-7241). Elodie B. Todd, half-sister of Mary Todd Lincoln, is among those remembered, as are William Rufus King and Congressman Benjamin Sterling.

The 1847 Smitherman Historic Building (109 Union Street, 334-874-2174) has served as a university, a Confederate hospital, a county courthouse, and a military school. It contains early memorabilia from the area.

While in Selma, take time to visit the Siegel Gallery (706 Broad Street, 334-875-1138). Located in a historic house, the gallery showcases regional and local artists.

Riverfront Park is the site of the Civil War Battle of Selma, which is re-enacted each April.

From Selma take US 41 to **Camden.** Located on a bend of the Alabama River, Camden was one of fifty steamboat landings along the river during the peak of cotton production. It was named by Dr. John D. Caldwell to honor his hometown of Camden, South Carolina.

The Old South town is characterized by delicate ironwork staircases, a solitary stone Confederate soldier, white clapboard churches, and a visual feast of architectural styles. Because the Civil War essentially ended with the burning of Selma, Camden's treasures have been preserved. Wilcox County has more buildings dating to the 1850s and earlier than does any other county in Alabama but Mobile County.

The most significant structure in Camden is the Wilcox Female Institute (301 Broad Street, 334-682-4929), built in 1850. One of the first schools for girls in the state, it attracted students from all over the South. Prior to that time girls were taught at home.

Two stories high, with two pairs of interior end chimneys, the structure features a central pedimented portico with two modified Doric columns and a second-floor suspended balcony, as well as the original belfry. Gone, however, are the large, central rear wing that served as a dormitory and classrooms, the frame breezeway, and the frame dining hall and kitchen. As time and money permit, these structures will be reconstructed. Today, the building houses a history museum and serves as a meeting place for cultural and civic organizations.

Drive by and admire the Dale Masonic Lodge on Broad Street. Built in 1857, the two-story structure features a pedimented portico and fanlights. The one-story clapboard Jones Law Office at Court and Water Streets, built about 1850, features a gabled roof, a pedimented porch with turned bracketed supports, fish-scale shingles, and ornamental saw work. The Wilcox County Public Library, located in the old courthouse (100 Broad Street, 334-682-4838), has an extensive Civil War genealogy library. Every other year the historical society sponsors a tour of historic homes and buildings.

Ebenezer Hearn, an early Wilcox County itinerant Methodist minister and veteran of the War of 1812, built a simple, two-story I-shaped home, now known as Gaines Ridge, in the 1830s (State 10, 334-682-9707). One of the few I-shaped structures surviving in rural Alabama, the absence of a center hallway coupled with its Federal-style interior indicate that the house predates the Greek Revival style of building popular in the 1840s and 1850s. This house was once the only two-story structure between Black's Bluff and Allenton, two early settlements fifty miles apart.

In 1898, the property was acquired by an ancestor of the Gaines family, which still owns it. This is the family of George Strother Gaines—Indian factor—and his brother General Edmund Pendleton Gaines, who captured Aaron Burr at McIntosh Bluffs and for whom Fort Gaines in Mobile Bay is named. Gainesville, Gainestown, and the antebellum mansion Gaineswood in Demopolis are all named in honor of the well-known brothers.

Today, Betty Gaines Kennedy uses the house as a restaurant: the GainesRidge Dinner Club serves dinner Wednesday through Saturday evenings. Betty's home cooking and lavish portions bring folks from as far away as Montgomery.

Reached by a long, tree-shaded drive dripping with Spanish moss, a front porch with comfortable rockers greets visitors and invites them to sit a spell. If you have to wait for a table, it's hard to decide whether to avail yourself of the front porch or to enjoy the view of the dependency buildings and woods beyond from the back deck.

Inside, the house retains the original plaster, wainscoting, and woodwork. Small, intimate rooms are furnished in a variety of styles. In the winter the log room is particularly cozy with its raised fireplace and player piano. Ask Betty to tell you the ghost stories associated with the house.

Pick up a guide for the Camden Cemetery Tour from the Wilcox Development Council (110 Court Street, 334-682-4929). Located just outside the cemetery gates on Broad Street is the Confederate Memorial. Efforts to raise funds for the monument began in 1866, and it was dedicated on Confederate Memorial Day, April 26, becoming the second memorial in Alabama to be dedicated to Confederate veterans.

Notable Camden citizens buried in the cemetery include Emmett Kilpatrick, who was an interpreter for Woodrow Wilson at Versailles and who as a Red Cross official was captured by the Bolsheviks in 1917; Alexander Bragg, a brother of Confederate general Braxton Bragg and the architect who built Camden's courthouse and many of its antebellum homes; Benjamin Meek Miller and Arthur Pendleton

Bagby, both governors of Alabama; and Ebenezer Hearn, who built GainesRidge. A pile of bricks marks the common grave of victims of the *Orline St. John,* a riverboat destroyed by fire in 1850.

Wilcox County is known for its good hunting. Hedgerows and thickets that border agricultural fields make good homes for quail, wild turkey, and white-tailed deer. Ducks are plentiful along the river.

Roland Cooper State Park (49 Deer Run Drive, 334-682-4838), located on the river, offers boat-launching ramps, public campgrounds, rental cabins, a country store, laundry, hiking trails, and a nine-hole golf course with a driving range and pro shop. The park has some rental boats, but you need your own motor.

The antebellum homes of Camden would be fertile ground for bed and breakfasts, but there are none. Places to stay include the Southern Inn (40 Camden Bypass, 334-682-4148), which has a restaurant, and the rustic Days Inn (39 Camden Bypass, 334-682-4555).

Camden is well-known for Joe C. Williams Pecans, a company that has been selling pecans and related products since 1952. (For mail orders call 334-682-4559.)

West of Camden on State 10 you will pass through the small, picturesque antebellum towns of **Pine Hill, Rosebud, Oak Hill, and Pine Apple,** as well as the outlying plantation homes in the surrounding countryside. A few hearty pioneers had already settled in the area known as The Ridge when Wilcox County was established in 1819. Early residents were Scotch-Irish Presbyterians who migrated from Abbeville, South Carolina, to the Alabama frontier. However, it was not until the mid-1840s that Oak Hill, Pine Hill, and Pine Apple came into being. Camden was established in 1842.

Generation after generation of the founding families has continued to live on lands settled by their ancestors. Periodic tours of historic homes allow visitors to see the insides of some of these grand homes. During the antebellum period, materials for the structures typically came from the property on which the house was constructed. Boards were cut from virgin pines. Clays and sand were combined to make bricks and plaster. Most of the basic construction was done by plantation slaves, but artisans were imported to create the elaborate plaster medallions, crown moldings, and cornices, or to create faux grains on floors, doors, and other wood trims.

Just beyond Pine Apple, in Forest Home, is a delightful country bed and breakfast, Pine Flat Plantation (334-346-2739). For more details see the Swing South chapter.

You'll not soon forget the Black Belt's gently flowing rivers, stark cliffs, and magnificent antebellum and Victorian homes; but above all you'll be warmed by the friendly people who are sure they live in heaven.

Wilcox Development Council, P.O. Box 369, Camden, AL 36726, 334-682-4929.

Wilcox Historical Society, P.O. Box 86, Camden, AL 36726, 334-682-4929.

CHAPTER 2

BRIDGING
THE GAPS

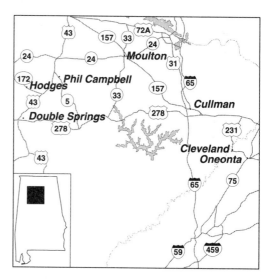

other Nature dominates the northwestern corner of Alabama, one of
the least inhabited regions of the
state. Just a few of the wonders to see
on this 212-mile trail are phenomenal natural
bridges, gloomy canyons, mysterious caverns,
vast forests, and tumultuous rapids. However,
there are also several small historic towns, the
greatest concentration of covered bridges in
the state, and numerous surprises.

Begin at Dismals Canyon near the town of **Phil Campbell,** off US 43 about 37 miles south of The Shoals area (Florence, Tuscumbia, Sheffield, and Muscle Shoals—see the Tennessee River Heritage Trail).

Brooding, mysterious, and steeped in legend, Dismals Canyon (205-993-4559) is well-known for its mysterious twinkle-in-the-dark worms called Dismalites. During the summer, night tours allow you to get the full impact of these strange worms glowing from the rocks to which they cling. Chickasaw Indians held secret rituals in the surrounding forest, and Aaron Burr and outlaws such as Jesse James hid out in the shadows. Named a National Natural Landmark, the canyon contains one of the oldest untouched forests east of the Mississippi, as well as exotic plants, natural bridges, unusual rock formations, sheer cliffs, cascading waterfalls, a limestone pool, hiking trails, and a rustic campground. You can canoe down Bear Creek, or, if you're more adventurous, you can challenge the Class I-IV rapids of the upper Bear. In the Old Country Store the ambiance is as ancient as the dust between the floorboards.

Go south on US 43 and turn west on State 72 to **Hodges.** Rock Bridge Canyon (205-935-3750) presents a panorama of natural bridges, waterfalls, unusual rock formations, flowers and plants.

Retrace State 172 and turn south on State 5 through **Haleyville.** Continue south on State 13 to US 278 at Natural Bridge. Then turn west and go to County 63, where a small park at Natural Bridge Resort of Alabama (US 278, 205-486-5330) surrounds an awe-inspiring sixty-foot-high and 148-foot-long double natural sandstone bridge that is the longest natural viaduct east of the Rockies, spanning forests, wilderness, and nature paths. Hike a short, easy path through a thick hemlock forest dating form the Ice Age to get to the base of the bridges and explore the hollowed-out cavern under them. A more strenuous trail through rocky bluffs leads to the top of the spans and Brushy Lake. Along the way be on the lookout for the twenty-seven varieties of ferns beside the trail. The 200-million-year-old spans were created when a stream eroded the sand-

Help yourself to a cola at the Country Store

stone away, leaving behind the iron-ore veins that now support the two giant arches. The resort features picnic areas, concession stands, and a gift shop.

Retrace US 278 east through Winston County to **Double**

Springs, located just at the edge of the William B. Bankhead National Forest (South Main Street, 205-489-4111). Named for actress Tallulah Bankhead's father who was a former Speaker of the House, the forest encompasses 180,000 acres teeming with natural attractions: bluffs, canyons, waterfalls, lakes, and four recreation areas.

Sipsey Wilderness on Cranal Road is the best known of the recreation areas and a 26,000-acre paradise for hikers and canoe fans. Its gorges, sandstone bluffs, cool canyons, flowing streams, and pine and hardwood virgin timberlands are bursting with exotic plants, rare birds, and mammals. A rock-rimmed box canyon has a vertical drop of 100 feet. You can fish in the Sipsey Branch of the Black Warrior River or hike along Bee Branch from Forest Road 208.

The other Bankhead National Forest recreation areas in which you can enjoy nature's wonders are Brushy Lake Recreation Area, which contains four hundred acres and a lake; Clear Creek Recreation Area, which has a lake, waterfalls, high bluffs, and a white sandy beach on its four hundred and twenty-five acres; and Houston Recreation Area adjacent to Lewis Smith Lake.

Double Springs is best known for an incident that occurred during the Civil War. The hill people, meeting at Looney's Tavern, led an unsuccessful struggle against Alabama's secession from the Union. They elected Christopher Sheats, a young schoolteacher, to attend the secession convention in Montgomery and cast their vote of opposition. Not only was his position defeated, he was also imprisoned for treason. Winston County demonstrated its independence from the Confederacy by forming the Free State of Winston.

The old tavern is gone now, but its remarkable story is told in a Civil War musical entitled "The Incident at Looney's Tavern," which is performed at Looney's Tavern Amphitheater and Theme Park (US 78 East, 205-489-5000 or 800-489-5017). The story (dramatized Thursday through Saturday evenings from May through October) is told with music, dance, and hill-country humor in the fifteen-hundred-seat outdoor theater overlooking Bankhead National Forest and Smith Lake.

Also part of the complex is Dual Destiny, an indoor theater where a rotating series of plays are performed throughout the year. One production uses state-of-the-art technology in the form of audio-animatronic Confederate and Union soldiers whose camp songs evoke the emotion, drama, and humor of the Civil War. The park also includes Sister Sarah's Kitchen restaurant, a miniature golf course, a gift shop, a deli, and an ice-cream parlor.

Looney's riverboat, *The Free State Lady*, is a sixty-passenger paddlewheeler that offers two-hour cruises on Lewis Smith Lake. Enjoy the scenic beauty, beautiful foliage, rugged cliffs, and mysterious cover of the Sipsey River and the Bankhead National Forest while master storytellers spin yarns and retell age-old legends about the hill country and the Free State of Winston.

Double Springs and Haleyville jointly host the Free State of Winston Festival in June.

From Double Springs take State 33 north through the Bankhead National Forest to **Moulton.** Animal House Zoological Park (2056 County 161, 205-974-8634) is an unusual park and breeding farm that features everything from African lions to red-ruffed lemurs. Moulton sponsors an Indian Festival in May and the Summerfest Antique and Classic Car Show in August.

From Moulton take State 157 south toward Cullman and turn south on County 1043 to the Clarkson Covered Bridge. Alabama's largest covered truss bridge sits in a pleasant, shady park where you can explore a dogtrot cabin and a grist mill.

Continue on County 1048 to US 278 and turn east. Pass through **Cullman** for now and go east from town on State 74 to Ave Maria Grotto (1600 Saint Bernard Drive, 205-734-4110). Known as Little Jerusalem, the garden contains more than a hundred and twenty-five miniatures of famous churches, shrines, and buildings from around the world, all perched on a hillside on the grounds of Alabama's first and only Benedictine Abbey. These miniatures are the result of forty years of work by Brother Joseph Zoettl, who came to the abbey from Bavaria in 1892.

A tiny man whose plans to be a priest were dashed by an injury, Zoettl became a brother instead and shoveled coal in the abbey's power plant for forty years. During his spare time, he used stone, cement, and scraps of anything else he could get his hands on to create miniatures of important buildings, mostly ones of religious significance. Ironically, he had seen only two of the original buildings in person; the rest he reconstructed from photos after extensive reading and study.

Initially, Brother Joseph used fragments he found around the abbey to create his Lilliputian buildings, which he then set out behind his workshop. Soon there were a great many miniatures, and their fame spread so far that visitors became an unwelcome intrusion. A nearby three-acre rock quarry was landscaped and turned into the new home of the miniatures.

As word of Brother Joseph's hobby spread, people from around the world began mailing him materials he might be able to use. He received so many marbles that the standing joke around the abbey was that Brother Joseph could "never lose his marbles." When the artisan was asked why he chose this unusual pastime, he replied, "I solve problems by miniaturizing them."

Brother Joseph built his last model, the Basilica of Lourdes, when he was eighty years old. He died in 1961, but his masterpiece is still seen by thousands of visitors each year and is listed in *Ripley's Believe It Or Not*. Get a brochure for the self-guided tour at the gift shop. It will identify St. Peter's Basilica, the Colosseum in Rome, the Leaning Tower of Pisa, the city of Jerusalem, Noah's Ark, the Tower of Babel, and the Hanging Gardens of Babylon, among others. The abbey also comprises the largest hand-cut stone church in northern Alabama, a prep school, a retreat center, and spartan bed-and-breakfast accommodations.

Return to town. The Cullman County Museum (211 Second Avenue NE, 205-739-1258) is a replica of the twin-turreted Victorian home of Cullman's founder, Colonel John G. Cullman. In 1873, he and five other families arrived from Germany and established a colony in northern Alabama. In addition to Colonel John Cullman's

Room featuring his own furniture, the museum contains a large quantity of pieces from the Cullman Archaeological Society that emphasize the town's German heritage.

The Archaeological Room features Native American artifacts including a seven-foot carving of a Native American warrior created from a sweet-gum tree. The Primitive Room contains turn-of-the-century tools, household items, and other fixtures of daily life. The Child's Room features toys and baby carriages. The South Room or Wall of Pictures is a photographic history of Cullman. Colonel Cullman is immortalized with a towering statue next to the museum. Main Street replicates the shops found in Cullman over a hundred years ago: a hobby shop, a dry-goods store, a drug store, a doctor's office, a general store, a jewelry shop, a book store, a photographic studio, a department store, and a gun shop. Window-shop for outfits from the 1850s at The Clothing Store.

Just around the corner is Weiss Cottage (First Avenue, 205-739-1258), the oldest house in the city and one-time home of the physician Dr. Aldo Weiss. Dr. Weiss was a prominent Cullman physician and accoucheur (what would now be known as an obstetrician) in the last quarter of the nineteenth century. He built this house in 1875.

Cullman has a busy festival schedule with a Bluegrass Superjam in April and November, the Bloomin' Festival in April, Classic Street Machines in July, and Oktoberfest in October.

North of Cullman, between Vinemont and Lacon, you can walk across a swinging bridge suspended over a waterfall at Hurricane Creek Park (US 31, 205-734-2125). Several miles of hiking trails pass natural stone sculptures. If you're tired, you can return by cable car.

Return to Cullman once again and continue south on US 31 to I-65 to Rickwood Caverns State Park near Warrior (370 Rickwood Park Road, 205-647-9692). The underground "miracle mile" is composed of extraordinary corridors and stunningly illuminated chambers highlighting thousands of twinkling white limestone formations. The park offers camping, swimming, miniature golf, hiking trails, and a miniature train ride.

Take State 160 north toward Cleveland. The greatest concentration of surviving covered bridges in Alabama is between Nectar and Oneonta, making the area the "Covered Bridge Capital" of Alabama.

On your way to Cleveland, about 14 miles from Warrior, is the small town of **Nectar** and the site of the Nectar Bridge, which spanned the Locust Fork of the Warrior River until it burned in 1993. It was the longest covered bridge in Alabama and the fourth longest in this country.

When you reach **Cleveland,** go 1.5 miles south of town on State 79 to the Swann Bridge. Built near the turn of the century, it is 324 feet long.

Return to Cleveland and go east on US 231 to Palisades Park (US 231, 205-589-2263). Located on Stone Bluff on 1,300-foot Mount Ebell, the park features two pioneer cabins, a schoolhouse, a farm museum, an arboretum, and nature trails. Scenic views are best seen from Inspiration Point.

Continue east on US 231 to the 95-foot-long Easley Bridge, which spans a creek whose banks are covered with wildflowers.

When you reach Oneonta, take State 75 north about 5-miles to Horton Mill Bridge, the first covered bridge in the South to be added to the National Register of Historic Places. At 220 feet above the creek, this covered bridge is the highest covered bridge above water in this country.

Return to **Oneonta.** The Blount County Memorial Museum (204 Second Street North, 205-589-2263) is a project of the Blount County Historical Society. Dedicated to all native Blount Countians who have served in wars, the museum contains Blount County history, genealogical research material, and covered-bridge art. The Edison Foundation's Collection of Edisonia contains the first handblown light bulbs, a phonograph and records, and china dolls. The museum's facade is constructed of old brick from Howard College in Birmingham.

Needless to say, Oneonta is the site of the Blount County Covered Bridge Festival in October.

As an alternative or supplemental route in northwest Alabama, you might want to explore the significant area south of the Tennessee River and north of the Bankhead National Forest in Lawrence County. Lawrence County Public Transportation (14980 Court Street, 205-974-2488) has developed two driving tours, the "Northern Historical Tour" which begins in Moulton and includes historic Courtland and Town Creek; and the "Southern Scenic Views" tour which begins west of Moulton at Muck City on State 24, then turns south on County 23 at Mt. Hope into the Bankhead National Forest.

From natural bridges to covered bridges, this region of northern Alabama spans the centuries and attracts visitors to enjoy the wilderness as well as the historic sites.

Blount County-Oneonta Chamber of Commerce, P.O. Box 87, Oneonta, AL 35121, 205-274-2153.

Courtland Town Hall, P.O. Box 106, Courtland, AL 35618, 205-637-2707.

Franklin County Chamber of Commerce, 500 North Jackson Avenue, Russellville, AL 35653, 205-332-1760.

Haleyville Area Chamber of Commerce, 1200 Twenty-first Street, Haleyville, AL 35565, 205-486-4611.

Lawrence County Public Transportation, 14980 Court Street, Moulton, AL 35650, 205-974-2488.

Winston County Tourism Association, c/o Handy Pack, US 278 West, Double Springs, AL 35553, 205-489-2414.

CHAPTER 3

CHATTA-HOOCHEE TRACE

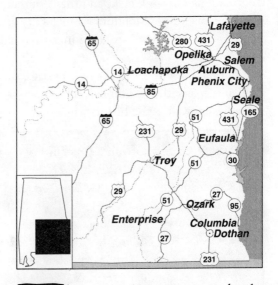

When a river serves as a border between two states, the dividing line is usually through the middle of the river. The Chattahoochee River separating Alabama and Georgia is an exception: the river belongs entirely to Georgia. Although the neighboring states may squabble about use of the waters in the river, the two states have formed a unique partnership to champion the scenic, historic, and recreational attractions on both banks of the river.

Identical legislation was passed by the Alabama Legislature and the Georgia General Assembly to form the Historic Chattahoochee Commission (HCC), which unites eighteen counties stretching from Auburn/Opelika in east-central Alabama south to the border of Alabama and the Florida Panhandle.

Founded in 1978, the HCC is the first and only tourism/preservation agency in the nation with the authority to cross state lines to pursue goals common to all the counties involved.

The Chattahoochee Trace is a pleasurable mixture of romantic Old South heritage and New South innovations. The 487-mile trail is a mecca for every type of vacationer: history buffs, campers, environmentalists, bird watchers, hunters, fishermen, cyclists, and bed-and breakfast-aficionados. The region is rich in lakes, championship golf courses, historic structures, and Native American sites, as well as phenomenal natural topography. The river is navigable from Phenix City to the Gulf of Mexico. Pilgrimages and festivals abound. Best of all, the area is easily accessible for day- to week-long trips. Some of the highlights can be seen on less than a tankful of gas.

When we explored the Chattahoochee Trace, we began in Eufaula—about a third of the way south into the Trace—and we touched on the highlights on both sides of the river in two grueling days of exploration. We spent one day on the Alabama side and one day on the Georgia side. Although we've proven the expedition possible, we don't recommend such a frenzied trip—there's too much to see and enjoy, too many exciting places at which to stay and eat, too many surprises that you'd like to linger over. We've described the attractions on the Georgia side of the river in our book, *Country Roads of Georgia* (Country Roads Press, 1995).

Here we explore the Alabama side of the Chattahoochee Trace from north to south, beginning with **Lafayette,** north of I-85 on US 431 and State 1, not far from the Alabama-Georgia border. The century-old Collins Drugstore (102 Lafayette Street, no phone) features medical memorabilia from the area, such as medicines, showcases, pharmacy containers, and dispensing bottles, as well as an old soda fountain, cash registers, and tobacco products. Lafayette's imposing 1899 Chambers County Courthouse, the centerpiece of the Courthouse Square Historic District, was featured in the movie *Mississippi Burning*.

From Lafayette drive south on US 431, then take State 147 south to **Auburn.** Encompassing the earliest portion of what is now Auburn University, the Auburn Historic District contains buildings that date from the 1850s to the early 1900s and reflect revivalist architectural styles of the period. The eclectic 1888 Victorian Samford Hall (South College Street), better known as Old Main, is the focal point of the campus. Pebble Hill, now the Auburn University Center for the Arts and Humanities (101 DeBardeleben Street), was the 1847 residence of one of the co-founders of the university. Built in 1851, the Auburn University Chapel is the oldest building in town. It once served as a Confederate hospital, and legend says that the ghost of a Confederate soldier appears periodically. Other historic buildings include the Flemish-style Smith Hall built in 1908, the Greek Revival Langdon Hall built in 1846, and the Romanesque Revival Hargis Hall built before 1920.

A popular fixture in Samford Park around Old Main is the historic Civil War lathe. Made in Selma for the manufacture of cannons for the Confederacy, it was buried for a time to prevent its capture by Union troops. Following the war, the lathe was used for decades in iron and steel mills before being presented to the university. Beyond the lathe is the Annie Terrell Basore Memorial Garden, a peaceful landscaped corner of the campus. The Donald E. Davis Arboretum on the campus is open to the public as well. You can see the school's mascot, Tiger—a golden eagle that serves as the War Eagle—in the aviary on the campus.

If you are staying in Auburn, you might enjoy the Crenshaw Guest House Bed and Breakfast (371 North College Street, 334-821-1131). The Victorian main house contains several spacious, high-ceilinged rooms furnished with antiques, and the contemporary guest house offers accommodations with kitchen facilities.

A celebrated gathering place for eating and browsing is Behind the Glass (168 East Magnolia Avenue, 334-826-1113), which offers light fare and a dessert bar. The interesting atmosphere is enhanced by changing art exhibits, a bookstore, and a boutique.

Take State 14 west to **Loachapoka** to see the Lee County Historical Museum (State 14, 334-887-5560). Housed in an old trade-center building, the museum is a repository of artifacts and memorabilia relating to Lee County and is open by appointment. Sixteen structures, including an old hotel and residential houses, are part of the Lee County historic district.

Retrace State 14 through Auburn and head east toward Opelika. Between the two towns, off County 97, is the Grand National golf course (see the Field of Greens chapter).

Opelika boasts the Opelika Historic Railroad District, where you can shop and eat in recently restored late nineteenth-century buildings or tour the 1896 Lee County Courthouse (South Ninth Street, 334-887-5560), a neoclassical brick courthouse that is unusually fine for a county that was so rural at the time the courthouse was built. The Museum of East Alabama (Ninth Street, 334-749-2751) houses hundreds of exhibits and books portraying the history of Alabama. Wander through the residential neighborhoods and admire the cornucopia of architectural styles, predominantly Greek Revival, Victorian, and American bungalow. The 1904 Queen Anne-style Whitfield-Searcy House (601 Avenue A, 334-745-4861 or 334-749-4711) serves as the Opelika Chamber of Commerce.

Stay at the magnificent Heritage House bed and breakfast (714 Second Avenue, 334-705-0485) and shop at the adjoining Carriage House gift shop.

Six miles south of town on Spring Villa Road the 1850 Gothic Revival house serves as the centerpiece of Spring Villa Park.

Nine miles east of Opelika on US 280/US 431 in **Salem** is the Salem-Shotwell Covered Bridge, one of only three "kissing bridges" (covered bridges where sweethearts could kiss without being seen) in the Chattahoochee Trace and the only one on the Alabama side.

Nearby, between Salem and Bleeker, is the A. D. McClain Museum (County Road 145, 334-745-7030). Constructed in 1910, the former doctor's office contains a drug store with a soda fountain and pharmacy—all restored—and is open by appointment.

Continue on US 280/US 431/State 1 to **Phenix City,** site of John Godwin's grave. The monument was erected by Horace King, a former slave of bridge-builder John Godwin. King himself went on to become a master bridge-builder. The marker was placed in "lasting remembrance of the love and gratitude he felt for his lost friend and former master."

Take US 431 south, then go south on State 165 to the Fort Mitchell National Cemetery (553 State 165, 334-855-4731). Known as the Arlington of the South, the cemetery is the final resting place for U.S. military veterans from World War I to the Gulf War. It is adjacent to the site of Fort Mitchell, which originally served as the U.S. agency for the Creek Indians. From 1836 to 1837, Native Americans were interned there before being removed to Oklahoma via the Trail of Tears.

Continue south on State 165, then turn west on County 18 to **Seale.** The Old Russell County Courthouse (one block east of US 431, 334-855-3123 or 334-855-3450), built in 1868, is the oldest courthouse in eastern Alabama and one of the oldest in the state.

Drive south on US 431/State 1 to **Eufaula,** which is a treasure trove of late-nineteenth-century architectural gems. Begin your exploration of Eufaula with Shorter Mansion (340 North Eufaula Avenue, 334-687-3793), Eufaula's visitors center. The 1906 neoclassical Greek Revival mansion contains antique furnishings, Confederate relics, and memorabilia from six Alabama governors.

Hart House (211 North Eufaula Avenue, 334-687-9755) is a restored 1850 one-story Greek Revival house that serves as the

The neoclassical Shorter Mansion in Eufaula was built in 1906

headquarters and visitor center for the HCC. The house contains some original furniture.

Drive by Sheppard Cottage (504 West Barbour Street), a private home. The 1837 raised Cape Cod cottage is the oldest residence in Eufaula.

In Eufaula stay at Kendall Manor (534 West Broad Street, 334-687-8847), a magnificent Italianate mansion.

Known as the Big Bass Capital of the World, Lake Eufaula has 640 miles of shoreline and an average depth of fifteen to eighteen feet. Stay at Lakepoint State Park Resort (US 431 North, 334-687-8011 or 800-544-5253). The park's accommodations range from primitive campsites to cottages to a resort inn that offers a pool, golf, tennis, and boating.

In the Eufaula area is a most unusual attraction—Tom Mann's Fish World (US 431 North, 334-687-3655). The complex includes a collection of Indian artifacts, a huge aquarium, a tombstone honoring Mann's favorite fish, and a shop that sells Mann's own fishing equipment. Challenge your fishing skills at Mann's eighteen-hole fishing course.

Eufaula National Wildlife Refuge (Old State 165, 334-687-4065) is a feeding and wintering habitat for waterfowl, birds of prey, songbirds, and other migratory birds. Marshes, forests, and uplands border the Walter F. George Reservoir on the Chattahoochee River.

Two major yearly events in Eufaula are the Eufaula Pilgrimage and Antique Show in April—which draws thousands to the small town—and the Summer Festival (in October) celebrating Native American heritage.

Leave Eufaula on US 431 South, then go west on State 30 to **Clayton,** where you'll find the Octagon House (103 North Midway Street, 334-775-8718), the only surviving antebellum octagonal house in Alabama. It is open by appointment only. In the cemetery across the street is the Whiskey Bottle Tombstone. The satirical head and foot stones of the grave marker are shaped like whiskey bottles and complete with removable lids. They were erected by W.T. Mullen's widow, who accused her late husband of drinking himself to death.

Although not on the Chattahoochee Trace, a detour to Troy is worth the extra time. From Clayton take State 51 south to Louisville, turn west on State 130 and take it to US 29, where you will turn west to **Troy.** Take US 231 South to visit the Pike Pioneer Museum (248 US 231 South, 334-566-3597), where ten thousand artifacts and demonstrations celebrate the folk culture of the nineteenth and early twentieth centuries.

Several historic structures sit on the museum's fifteen acres of wooded land. Housed in the museum building are the agricultural wing, the household wing, a print shop, and a typical pioneer street. The agricultural wing contains antique farm implements, a horse-drawn hearse, and a moonshine still.

In the pioneer home wing you'll see articles that were in common use during the Alabama frontier period. Items in the collection range from pegged pie safes to an elegant piano, and volunteers produce authentic handwoven goods on an overhead loom.

A news press, linotype machine, children's corner, and other displays are contained in the print shop. The pioneer street features a doctor's office, a bank, and barber shop, in addition to antique road machinery, mile-post markers, and hitching posts.

Moved intact to the museum grounds, the Adams General Store still contains much of its original equipment and a small post office. It is stocked as it might have been in the 1920s.

Other structures moved to the grounds include a board-and-batten tenant house, a dogtrot split-log house filled with handmade farmhouse antiques, a caretaker's house, a replica of a well, an authentic privy, and an old windmill. Guides give demonstrations of weaving, spinning, quilting, and needlework. The House of Dunn's (204 South Brundidge Street, 334-566-9414) offers bed-and-breakfast accommodations.

The southern area of the Trace is known as the Wiregrass Region because the native grass is noted for its tough, wiry roots. Because of the region's temperate weather, undulating plains, and gentle hills, it is perfect for the cultivation of peanuts—the number-one source of farm income in the tri-state area of Alabama, Georgia, and Florida.

From Troy take US 231 south and make a short jog east on State 27 to **Ozark,** where you can visit the Claybank Church (East Andrews Avenue, 334-774-9321), which is the oldest original hand-hewn log church in Ozark/Sale County. Workmen used stumps for its foundation, and the church's board shingles were split by hand. Built in 1852, the church was once the center of community religious, social, and political life. The wooden pulpit and original benches survive.

When the Greek Revival Mizell Mansion (409 East Broad Street, 334-774-9323) was built in 1912 by J.D. Holman, a horse and mule trader, ornamental work was specified but never completed. When H. Jack Mizell restored the house in 1982, he completed the ornamentation in addition to adding modern conveniences.

From Ozark swing southwest on State 27 to Fort Rucker, home of the U.S. Army Aviation Museum (Andrews Avenue and Novosel Street, 334-255-4443 or 334-255-4584). Tracing the history of Army aviation from the beginning, the facility contains a hundred and fifty aircraft, as well as the world's largest collection of helicopters. The collection includes many one-of-a-kind aircraft and research and development experiments in both fixed-wing and rotor-wing flight. Of special note are *Army One*, President Dwight D. Eisenhower's helicopter, and the C-121A Constellation aircraft *Bataan* used by General Douglas MacArthur during the Korean War. The museum also contains an extensive collection of World War I aircraft and a 1909 Bleriot—a single-seat tractor monoplane. Introduced at the first Paris Aero Salon, it is the smallest practical monoplane ever built.

Continue on State 27 to **Enterprise.** The town's most cherished landmark—the Boll Weevil Monument on Main Street—is the world's only monument to the voracious pest. In 1915 the boll weevil devoured two-thirds of Coffee County's cotton crop. Faced with ruin, local farmers were forced to diversify. As a result, the county is now the Peanut Capital of the World, so citizens wanted to thank the boll weevil.

The Enterprise Welcome Center (US 84 Bypass, 334-393-3977) is located inside a replica of an early nineteenth-century log cabin. Nearby, the Little Red Schoolhouse, also a replica, contains authentic desks, school books, chalkboards, and a pot-bellied stove.

At the Depot Museum (Railroad Street, 334-393-2901), a 1903

Atlantic Coast Railroad station, you can peruse an extensive collection of artifacts relating to the Wiregrass Region. Two waiting rooms contain Native American relics and early twentieth-century medical equipment and books, as well as exhibits pertaining to the legal profession. The centerpiece of the legal memorabilia is a huge judicial bench that was once in the courtroom of the old Coffee County Courthouse. Diverse displays such as cornerstones, school items, and industry mock-ups fill the stationmaster's office.

However, the bulk of the items are contained in the large freight warehouse in which murals depicting early life in the area adorn the walls. A clothing exhibit features apparel that once belonged to Enterprise's first citizens. Antique agricultural items are displayed in an extension to the warehouse.

From Enterprise take State 134/State 92/State 12 to **Dothan.** Among the architecturally significant structures in town is the 1915 Dothan Opera House (103 North Street, 334-793-0128), a neoclassical building with Italian Renaissance influences. Admire the 1907 Dixie Train Depot.

At the Wiregrass Museum of Art (126 North College Street, 334-794-3871) you can see changing exhibits every six weeks. In addition to displaying the works of local schoolchildren, the museum has a wonderful hands-on gallery for youngsters.

Across the street in Poplar Head Park is the Mule Marker, a monument which recognizes the role the mule played in the development of the Wiregrass region. After the Civil War, rich planters had to tend their farms without slaves. Poor whites and freed blacks had to farm without much, if any, help. In addition, many horses had been killed during the war. The mule made plowing and planting much easier for a small number of people to do. The Wiregrass Region is the only place that erected a monument to the animal.

Mus-quoian, an oak sculpture on the lawn of the Love Memorial Library, was carved by Hungarian immigrant Peter Toth, who has carved similar sculptures in all fifty states. His purpose is to remind everyone of the oppression suffered by Native Americans.

North of town on US 431 you can discover the natural and cultural heritage of the Wiregrass Region in the sixty-acre Landmark Park (US 431 North, 334-794-3452). In addition to the farmstead—a living-history museum of a typical turn-of-the-century farm complete with barns, cribs, sheds, livestock, and gardens—the park features the 1908 Headland Presbyterian Church, the Square for the Arts used as a setting for concerts and special events, nature trails, wildlife exhibits, boardwalks over beaver ponds, an Interpretive Center, and a planetarium.

Farther north on US 431 at **Headland** is the Auburn University Peanut Experiment Station. With six hundred acres it is the world's largest such facility and is on the cutting edge of new agricultural frontiers.

From Headland take State 134 east to **Columbia.** For a journey into the technological present and future, visit the Farley Nuclear Visitors Center (State 95 South, 334-899-5108), which presents the story of energy from pre-historic times to the nuclear age. Start with a movie about energy, then try your skill at one of many hands-on displays. Use muscle power to generate electricity on a treadmill generator or match wits with computers and examine the control-room simulator.

Historic sites to drive by include the imposing 1890 Purcell-Killingsworth House (North Main Street) and the Old Columbia Jail (North Street), a wooden prison built in 1862.

Take State 95 south to the extreme southern end of the Chattahoochee Trace—the Scenic Forks area that marks the spot where the Chattahoochee and Flint Rivers meet and flow into man-made Lake Seminole in Florida. In addition to the recreational activities associated with the lake and Chattahoochee State Park, many historic attractions and unique architectural styles provide entertainment for everyone.

From the Alabama-Florida border retrace State 95 north to **Abbeville,** the oldest remaining colonial settlement in east

Alabama. The town is older than both Henry County and the state of Alabama. Drive around to see the many interesting turn-of-the-century commercial and residential buildings. Farther north on State 95 is the Walter F. George Lock and Dam on Lake Eufaula. This structure is the second highest lock-lift east of the Mississippi. Continue north to Eufaula and the end of the tour. The Chattahoochee Trace takes you from the mule age to the nuclear age. If your interest has been piqued, set aside another trip to explore the Georgia side of the river.

We highly recommend that you study the brochure called "Chattahoochee Trace: Mini-Tour Guide," which is available from the HCC. This brochure divides the Chattahoochee Trace into manageable segments according to location or interest focus. It includes maps, visitor information and welcome center locations, bed and breakfasts, historic restaurants, marinas and boating facilities, U.S. Army Corps of Engineers Public Use Areas, sites on the National Register of Historic Places, National Historic Landmarks, hunting lodges, and a calendar of events. The guide is an invaluable source of information on days and hours of operation, admission charges, and directions to the attractions.

Auburn-Opelika Convention and Visitors Bureau, 714 East Glenn Avenue, Auburn, AL 36831, 334-887-8747 or 800-321-8880.

Eufaula/Barbour County Tourism Council, 102 North Orange Street, Eufaula, AL 36072-1055, 334-687-5283 or 800-524-7529.

Historic Chattahoochee Commission, P.O. Box 33, Eufaula, AL 36072-0033, 334-687-9755.

Houston Welcome Center (US 231 North of Florida state line), 15121 US 231, Slocomb, AL 36375, 334-677-5042.

Lanett Welcome Center, I-85, Valley, AL 36854, 334-576-8574.

CHAPTER 4

THE ROAD TO CIVIL RIGHTS

lthough the 1960s saw spontaneous
eruptions of civil disobedience
throughout the South, Alabama is
the acknowledged forerunner of the
Civil Rights movement. Shocking images of
that period are etched forever into our minds:
cross burnings, white-sheeted figures,
marchers on a bridge being beaten to the
ground by troopers wielding billy clubs and
whips, young people being set upon by snap-

ping dogs and powerful water hoses. The sites along this 300-mile trail (Selma, Montgomery, Birmingham, Old Cahawba, and Tuskegee) all played important roles in making civil-rights history. Today, memorials in these cities seek to heal years of anguish and educate a new generation.

Alabama has been home to many prominent black Americans— W.C. Handy, Booker T. Washington, George Washington Carver, Jesse Owens, Marva Collins, General Daniel "Chappie" James, and Nat King Cole; but perhaps best remembered and honored are those African Americans such as Rosa Parks and Dr. Martin Luther King Jr. who spawned the Civil Rights movement.

What became an unstoppable tide started simply enough in **Montgomery** on December 1, 1955, when Rosa Parks, a tired black seamstress, made an earth-shattering decision: She refused to give up her seat on a city bus to a white man. This determined action resulted in her arrest. This incident served as the catalyst for the year-long, eventually successful Montgomery bus boycott and subsequent civil-rights crusade.

Martin Luther King Jr.'s first pastorate was what is now the Dexter Avenue King Memorial Baptist Church (454 Dexter Avenue, 334-263-3970), where he served from 1954 to 1960. It was here, near the capitol, that he began his leadership as the driving force behind the civil-rights struggle, using non-violent civil disobedience to further the cause of social reform. After many rallies at the church, King led the bus boycott which ended when the U.S. Supreme Court ruled that African Americans had the right to equal access to public transportation. A mural on the lower level of the church portrays the momentous events in the civil-rights effort and in King's life.

Before the Civil War, Court Square was the scene of auctions which included not only cotton and land, but also slaves. Ironically, it was from here that Rosa Parks boarded her fateful bus ride. Demonstrators participating in the Selma to Montgomery march in 1965 passed this square on their way to the capitol, where King addressed the exhausted marchers.

Dexter Avenue King Memorial Baptist Church where Martin Luther
King Jr. served as pastor from 1954 to 1960

The soaring staircases inside the imposing, white marble Alabama
State Capitol (Bainbridge Street and Dexter Avenue, 334-242-3750)
are the work of Horace King, a noted black contractor and bridge

builder. The slave of a bridge builder, King learned the trade. After the Civil War, King remained with his former master. When the master died, King continued to build bridges, homes, and government buildings and worked on other engineering projects. The Alabama State Capitol was the scene of many demonstrations throughout the civil-rights battle. (For more details about the Capitol, see the Swing South chapter.)

At the intersection of Dexter Avenue and Washington Avenue, black granite and water combine to form the haunting Civil Rights Memorial designed by Maya Lin, who is renowned for her design of the Vietnam War Memorial in Washington, D.C. Situated on the property of the Southern Poverty Law Center (400 Washington Avenue, 334-264-0286), the memorial has a central theme taken from King's passage ". . . until justice rolls down like waters and righteousness like a mighty stream."

Montgomery contains forty sites of significance to tracing black heritage in Alabama. Centennial Hill Historic District, centering on Jackson and High Streets, began in 1876 and remains a prominent black neighborhood. The North Lawrence–Monroe Street Historic District was the major black business district that emerged after the passage of the Jim Crow laws in the late nineteenth century.

The Alabama Department of Archives and History (624 Washington Avenue, 334-242-4443)—the nation's oldest state archives—displays a collection of paintings honoring famous Alabamians that includes those prominent blacks listed in this chapter. (The archives contain many other fascinating artifacts relating to Alabama's history—see the Swing South chapter.) Photographs and other exhibits about the Civil Rights movement in Montgomery are on display at the World Heritage Museum (119 West Jeff Davis Avenue, 334-263-7229), which is open by appointment.

The Cole-Samford House (1524 St. John Street) was the birthplace and early childhood home of Nat King Cole. The Jackson Community House (409 South Jackson Street) is associated with Jefferson Franklin Jackson, who was a black attorney active in the 1850s. It has served as a home for the elderly, an orphanage, and as the only library available to the black community. Today, it houses the Federation of Women and Youth Clubs.

Although the following homes are not open to the public, it is still worthwhile to drive by the home of Nathan Alexander (503 Union Street), a noted Reconstruction Republican; the Dorsett-Phillips House (422 Union Street), home of Montgomery's first black physician; the John W. Jones House (341 South Jackson Street), residence of the Reconstruction senator; the Dr. E. D. Nixon Home (647 Clinton Street), dwelling place of the civil-rights pioneer who posted bond for Rosa Parks; and the Dexter Avenue Baptist Church Pastorium (309 South Jackson Street), home of Dr. King during his ministry.

Significant black churches include the Bethel Baptist Church (2106 Mill Street); Beulah Baptist (3703 Rosa Parks Avenue); Church of the Good Shepherd (493 South Jackson Street); Congregational Christian (Union and High Streets); Day Street Baptist (861 Day Street); First Baptist (347 North Ripley Street); First Colored Presbyterian (310 North Hull Street); Holt Street Baptist (903 South Holt Street); Mount Zion African Methodist Episcopal Zion (657 South Holt Street); Old Ship A.M.E. Zion (483 Holcombe); Saint Paul Methodist (404 South Ripley); and Saint John A.M.E. (807 Madison Avenue).

Alabama State University (809 South Jackson) began in 1874 as the State Normal School and University for Colored Students and Teachers. On the campus at the Levi Watkins Learning Arts Center is the Dr. E. D. Nixon Collection, which consists of the civil-rights pioneer's papers, letters, and commendations.

Once the site of the Industrial School and the Booker T. Washington Elementary School, the Montgomery Industrial School now serves as the Montgomery Teacher Center, where adult education classes are offered. The Swayne School Site (Union and Grove Streets), is the site of a school organized for freed slaves by the American Missionary Association and the Freedmen's Bureau following the Civil War.

Prominent white city officials and black boycott leaders met in the roof-garden restaurant of the Ben Moore Hotel (Jackson and High Streets). Roots & Wings (1345 Carter Hill Road) houses an art gallery, theater, and book store all showcasing black painting and graphic arts.

Take I-65 north, then State 14 west to **Selma.** Dr. King said of the city in 1965: "Confrontation of good and evil compressed in the tiny community of Selma generated the massive power to turn the whole nation to a new course." Speaking about the Selma-to-Montgomery marches, President Lyndon B. Johnson remarked: "At times, history and fate meet at a single place to shape a turning point in man's unending search for freedom. So it was at Lexington and Concord. So it was a century ago at Appomattox. So it was last week in Selma."

Enter Selma over the infamous Edmund Pettus Bridge. Although the bridge is named for a Civil War hero, it earned its bad reputation as the place where protestors were attacked by troopers on Bloody Sunday, March 7, 1965. On March 9 another attempt was turned back without bloodshed. Twelve days later the South's largest civil-rights march successfully crossed the bridge with a National Guard escort and reached Montgomery on March 25, 1965. Five months later President Lyndon B. Johnson signed the Voting Rights Act into law.

The marches actually began at Brown Memorial A.M.E. Church (410 Martin Luther King Jr. Street, 334-874-7897), a 1907 Byzantine church which served as the local headquarters of the Civil Rights movement. Founded in 1867, it was the first A.M.E. church in the state. One room is dedicated to Dr. King, and a bust of the leader sits in front of the church, which is part of the walking tour of the area.

Get a brochure for the walking tour from the Selma–Dallas County Chamber of Commerce (513 Lauderdale Street, 334-875-7241). Ironically, the Martin Luther King Jr. Street historic district runs from Selma Avenue to Jeff Davis Avenue. At the opposite end of Martin Luther King Jr. Street is the Old Depot Museum (4 Martin Luther King Jr. Street, 334-874-2197), which contains exhibits of historical artifacts from the Civil War through the civil-rights strife.

Also located on Martin Luther King Jr. Street, First Baptist Church was the site of mass meetings and demonstrations. Built in 1894, it was designed by a local black architect and is considered one of the finest nineteenth-century examples of black churches in the state. Along Martin Luther King Jr. Avenue twenty memorials tell stories of the movement in Selma through words and searing pictures of individuals known and unknown, rich and poor, black and white, who came together for a common cause.

Other sites of interest on the walking tour include the Reformed Presbyterian Church (625 Jeff Davis Avenue), starting point of the Concerned White Citizens March in March 1965; the Dallas County Courthouse (Alabama and Lauderdale Streets), destination of most protest marches in an effort to register to vote; Tabernacle Baptist Church (1431 Broad Street), site of the first mass meeting on voting rights in Dallas County in 1963; and the Cecil C. Jackson Jr. Public Safety Building (1300 Alabama Avenue), a city and county jail in which Dr. King and other protestors were imprisoned in 1965.

Opened in 1993, the National Voting Rights Museum and Institute (1012 Water Avenue overlooking the Edmund Pettus Bridge, 334-418-0800) houses living history in the form of first-hand accounts of participants in many of the momentous events. *Footprints to Freedom* is an exhibit featuring plaster casts of the footprints of participants in the march to Montgomery.

Long before the Civil Rights movement, Selma had a proud black heritage. During Reconstruction Selma employed its first black policeman in 1867 and elected its first black judge in 1874. Ex-slave Benjamin S. Turner became the first Selmian elected to the U.S. House of Representatives in 1870. As Alabama's first black congressman he sought amnesty for Confederate leaders as well as civil rights for freed blacks. He is buried in Live Oak Cemetery. Jeremiah Haralson served as the first black Republican national committeeman in 1876.

Important black schools in Selma include Concordia College (1804 Green Street) and Selma University (Lapsley and Jeff Davis Streets), both junior colleges.

Striking murals of black life adorn the Wilson Building (Franklin Street). Rose Hill Cemetery (Beloit Road) is the burial ground for many ex-slaves. Live Oak Cemetery contains the remains of many slaves and prominent residents of Selma.

From Selma take State 22 west to County 9, then go five miles south to **Old Cahawba,** Alabama's first state capital (1820-1826) and a prosperous antebellum river town. It became a seat of black political power during Reconstruction, then finally a ghost town. Today, it is an important archaeological site with picturesque ruins.

Repeated flooding caused the capital to be moved to Tuscaloosa in 1826, and Old Cahawba was nearly abandoned. However, it recovered as a social and commercial center, a major distribution point for cotton shipped down the Alabama River, and a railroad boom town.

Then bad luck followed. During the Civil War the railroad was torn up by Union soldiers, an appalling prison holding three thousand Union soldiers was formed, and a flood once again inundated the town. In 1866 the county seat was moved to Selma and within ten years even the houses had been dismantled and moved.

During Reconstruction the abandoned courthouse was the scene of meetings of freedmen seeking to establish a base of political power. A new rural community of seventy former slave families created what was to become known as the Mecca of the Radical Republican party. However, even that community eventually disappeared. By 1900 almost no buildings remained.

Today, nature has reclaimed much of Old Cahawba, but you can stroll down the abandoned streets, explore the moss-covered ruins, read interpretive signs, and maybe talk to an archaeologist hard at work there. Begin with the Welcome Center (Beech and Capitol Streets), where exhibits feature artifacts and photographs.

Columns and chimneys mark old house sites. Gravestones tell the stories of forgotten people—just pick up a free guide to the cemetery. Old-fashioned roses and bulbs still bloom.

Important black history sites include Walnut Street, a place of stables, workshops, and mechanics; a slave exchange at Walnut and

North Streets; an infirmary for blacks; the courthouse on Vine Street where slaves were auctioned and where later freedmen attended political rallies and Congressman Haralson gave his re-election speech (Congressman Haralson was a black Congressman elected during Reconstruction. He ran for re-election in 1876, and during a speech, the white sheriff demanded that Haralson recant some of the things he was saying. When Haralson refused he was arrested and dragged off to jail. Haralson lost the election, other blacks were afraid to run for office, and the event spelled the doom of Reconstruction in Dallas County. Another black was not elected to office for almost a hundred years.); Babcock's Warehouse, which served as a church for blacks; the Colored Methodist Episcopal Church; and a bridge at the end of Oak Street, built by ex-slave Horace King. Two former slave residences survive and are now private homes not open to the public.

Hike the Clear Creek Nature Trail. The shaded picnic area has grills and restrooms. There's also a boat launch and excellent fishing. On the second Saturday in May Old Cahawba comes back to life for the Old Cahawba Festival, which features music, games, living history, storytelling, arts and crafts, and southern barbecue.

Return to State 22 and take it north to I-65, where you will turn north to **Birmingham,** a city of such turmoil in the 1960s that King called it "the most segregated city in America." Today a whole six-block district is dedicated to the memory of those events.

Kelly Ingram Park (Sixth Avenue North at Sixteenth Street) is dedicated as "A place of revolution and reconciliation." During the Civil Rights movement it was the focal point of grassroots resistance rallies. The Freedom Walk through the park features chilling sculptures of snarling dogs, water cannons pummeling demonstrators, and children being jailed. However, all paths lead to the center of the park, where a statue of Martin Luther King Jr. and a long pool in black marble create a peaceful, meditative oasis in stark contrast to these violent scenes.

Surrounding the park are the Sixteenth Street Baptist Church, the Birmingham Civil Rights Institute, the Alabama Jazz Hall of Fame, and several notable black businesses and eateries.

In 1963, the Sixteenth Street Baptist Church (1530 Sixth Avenue North, 205-251-9402) tragically burst into international prominence when a bomb killed four little girls attending Sunday School. The fatal explosion became a rallying cry for unity among blacks and concerned whites around the country. The church later served as the headquarters for mass meetings and demonstrations. A large stained-glass window memorializes the girls. Visitors and worshippers of all races are welcome.

Across the street is the Birmingham Civil Rights Institute (520 Sixteenth Street North, 205-328-9696), where you can explore the history of the Civil Rights movement from post-World War I racial segregation to present-day racial progress. A series of galleries includes the Barriers Gallery, the Confrontation Gallery, the Movement Gallery, and the Processional Gallery. Walkways are inclined in order to depict the uphill struggle for civil rights. An awe-inspiring journey on the road to equality, the trip begins with a film on Birmingham's history and segregation. Life-like figures, sound effects, and detailed exhibits offer slices of everyday life as well as pivotal incidents. Dramatic moments are retold on film in four mini-theaters. The journey ends in a gallery filled with exhibits depicting contemporary human-rights violations and triumphs throughout the world.

Housed in the historic Carver Theater for the Performing Arts, the Alabama Jazz Hall of Fame (Fourth Avenue North at Seventeenth Street, 205-254-2731) honors great jazz artists such as Nat King Cole, Duke Ellington, Lionel Hampton, and Erskine Hawkins who have ties to Alabama. Visitors travel from the beginnings of boogie-woogie to the jazz space journeys of Sun Ra and his Intergalactic Space Arkestra.

Most of the hundred and seventy original inductees to the Alabama Jazz Hall of Fame were students of John T. "Fess" Whatley at the old Birmingham Industrial School. Whatley was honored by *Jazz Monthly* in London as a "Maker of Musicians."

Interactive TV allows visitors to learn about specific performers, instruments, bands, and other facets of jazz. Classes for young musicians and numerous performances are among the regular activities at the Alabama Jazz Hall of Fame.

The neighborhood along Fourth Avenue between Fifteenth and Eighteenth Streets was a prosperous black business district in the early 1900s. Forced out of other areas by Jim Crow segregation, black businessmen established a commercial, social, and cultural center here. Black-owned banks, mortuaries, movie theaters, and nightclubs flourished through the sixties and are experiencing a resurgence today.

Stop for a bite to eat at Hosie's (321 Seventeenth Street North, 205-326-3495), one of these revitalized businesses. For barbecue or fish, Hosie's can't be beat. Pig ears and croaker (a type of fish) are specialties. While you're eating, get Hosie to share his upbeat philosophy of life with you.

In addition to the Civil Rights and Fourth Avenue Districts, two other districts are significant to black heritage. The Joseph Riley Smith Historic District, centering on Tenth Street and Ninth Court West, is the core of residential housing in the 1886 subdivision built for prominent members of the Smith family and their corporate and professional colleagues. Sixty-four houses of various nineteenth- and twentieth-century styles remain. The Smithfield Historic District, Eighth Avenue to Third Street West, was carved from the Joseph Riley Smith plantation in 1886. By 1898 it was the fourth-largest suburban community surrounding Birmingham. Streets were named for Smith's sons and grandsons, and avenues were named for their wives, daughters, and friends.

Career highlights of some of Alabama's greatest black sports figures are showcased at the Alabama Sports Hall of Fame (2150 Civic Center Boulevard, 205-323-6665). Joe Louis, Jesse Owens, Hank Aaron, Willy Mays, and Billy Williams are among those honored.

Some churches you might want to see include Pilgrim Lutheran (447 First Street North), Sixth Avenue Baptist (Martin Luther King Drive), and Trinity Baptist (328 Fourth Court North). Important buildings to drive by include the Alabama Penny Savings Bank

Building (310 Eighteenth Street North), which was the first black-owned bank in the state and the second largest in the country; the Dr. A.M. Brown House (319 North Fourth Terrace), residence of the black physician who founded World Health Week and now the Birmingham Art Club; the City Federation of Women's Clubhouse (551 Jasper Road), which once housed orphans and the elderly but now serves as a day nursery for the underprivileged; A.G. Gaston Gardens (1501 Fifth Avenue North), which was once the only first-class motel for blacks and a march assembly point and is now a home for the elderly and handicapped; Ruth B. Jackson Cottage (1301 Thirtieth Street North), home of the founder of the Alabama Association of Modern Beauticians; and the Windham Construction Company Office Building (528 Eighth Avenue), which housed a company noted for its construction of homes and public buildings.

No tour of black heritage sites would be complete without a pilgrimage to **Tuskegee.** Take I-65 south to Montgomery, then I-85 east. From I-85 exit onto State 81 south. Turn right at the intersection of State 81 and Old Montgomery Road and follow the signs.

Tuskegee University was formed in 1881 when a bill generated by a former slave and a former slave owner was passed by the Alabama Legislature to establish a school for blacks in Macon County. Although the bill provided $2,000 for teacher's salaries, no money was allotted for land, buildings, or equipment, so classes began with thirty students in a dilapidated church. A rural extension program took progressive ideas and training to many who could not attend classes on campus. Smaller schools and colleges founded and staffed by Tuskegee alumni sprang up around the South. Today Tuskegee University has grown to a hundred and sixty-one buildings on two hundred and sixty-eight acres with an academic community of five thousand students, faculty, and staff.

Booker T. Washington and George Washington Carver are the two black men associated with the institute above all others. Both were born into slavery—Washington before the Civil War started and Carver just before it ended. As freedmen, both labored at various menial jobs to make enough money to get an education.

Begin your tour with the Tuskegee Institute National Historic Site (1212 Old Montgomery Road, 334-727-3200). Located on the Tuskegee University campus, the site includes The Oaks, Booker T. Washington's home when he served as president of the college; the George Washington Carver Museum; and twenty-seven other landmarks. The Visitor Orientation Center is located in the Carver Museum. Follow the audio-visual presentation with a self-guided or guided tour of the museum.

The museum is divided into two sections: One area is devoted to Dr. Carver, and the other relates the growth and development of Tuskegee Institute and highlights such programs as agricultural extension work and the compilation of statistics on black life.

George Washington Carver came to work as head of the newly created Agriculture Department at Tuskegee University in 1896 and served there for forty-seven years. His advances with peanuts and other southern crops earned him the distinction of Fellow of the Royal Society in 1917.

Established in 1938 during the professor's lifetime, the Carver Museum contains Carver's personal belongings such as needlework, textile art, and paintings, as well as native plants, minerals, and birds, and the results of some of his scientific experiments.

Booker T. Washington was the first president of the institute. In 1899 a home was built for the president on property owned by him. Designed by Robert Taylor, the first black graduate of the Massachusetts Institute of Technology, the house was built by Tuskegee students. Even the bricks were made by students and faculty. The imposing Victorian structure was the first house in the area to have electricity. Now a museum operated by the National Park Service, the house is outfitted with functional furniture created by students and with ornate pieces obtained on Washington's worldwide travels, as well as with personal memorabilia. Check the schedule for guided tours.

About his house Washington said, "The actual sight of a first class house that a Negro has built is ten times more potent than

At the Carver Museum you can learn about George Washington Carver's experiments with southern crops

pages of discussion about a house that he ought to build, or perhaps could build."

Other campus attractions include the Washington Collection and Archives, found in the Library, which contains many books by and about blacks; the Administration Building (originally Booker T. Washington's office), which houses the Centennial Vision Mural; University Cemetery, where Washington, his family, Carver, and other noted persons associated with the university are buried; and the Booker T. Washington Monument, which depicts Washington "lifting the veil of ignorance" from his fellow blacks.

Although Grey Columns (399 Old Montgomery Road), the present home of the university president, is not open to the public, you should still drive by to admire the 1857 two-story Greek Revival mansion that features an octagonal cupola, six chimneys, and a columned portico.

Daniel "Chappie" James, a Tuskegee graduate, was America's first black four-star general. The Daniel "Chappie" James Center for Aerospace Science and Health Education houses the university's Army and Aerospace Sciences, Department of Aerospace Engineering, Natatorium, Health Education Department, and a memorial to General James.

Off the university campus, the Butler Chapel A.M.E. Zion Church (102 North Church Street) was the first site of Tuskegee University. The 1907 Romanesque Macon County Courthouse (Courthouse Square) features unique tower gargoyles combining a dragon with an eagle. The Veteran's Administration Medical Center (North Tuskegee) was the only hospital in the country for black veterans of World War I.

Moton Field/Tuskegee Army Air Field (Tuskegee Municipal Airport off Chappie James Drive) is known as the Home of Black Aviation, because World War II fighter pilot C. Alfred Anderson founded a school of aviation there and became its chief instructor. The school sponsors an annual Fly-In.

On US 80 east of Tuskegee is Taska, a replica of the cabin where Booker T. Washington was born. Crossing the picnic area is an 8.5-mile section of the Bartram Trail, named in honor of the eighteenth-century journeys of naturalist William Bartram.

The Alabama Bureau of Tourism and Travel has created several black heritage tours. "Trails of Higher Learning" is a four-day trip that includes visits to Alabama A&M University and Oakwood College in Huntsville, Talladega College in Talladega, Miles College in Fairfield, Stillman College in Tuscaloosa, Concordia College and Selma University in Selma, Alabama State University in Montgomery, and Tuskegee University.

"Two Centuries of Black History" is a seven-day tour that includes sites in Mobile, Carlton, Selma, Whitehall, Montgomery, Tuskegee, Birmingham, Decatur, Florence, and Muscle Shoals.

The "Martin Luther King Jr. Pilgrimage" is a two-day swing through Birmingham, Selma, and Montgomery.

The five-day "Famous Faces and Historic Places" includes the W. C. Handy Home and Museum and other sites in Florence, Coleman Hill in Athens, the gravesite of Harry the Slave in Marion, and significant landmarks in Decatur, Birmingham, Tuscaloosa, Selma, Montgomery, and Tuskegee.

Annually seventy-five fairs, festivals, and other special events honor black heritage.

For more information on myriad other black heritage sites throughout Alabama, contact the Alabama Bureau of Tourism and Travel for the guide "Alabama's Black Heritage."

While you are visiting the above cities and towns to explore their black heritage sites, take advantage of the many other attractions each offers. Birmingham's diversions are described in the Talladega to Tuscaloosa chapter, Selma is covered in the Black Belt chapter, and Montgomery in the Swing South chapter. These cities combine an intriguing blend of the charm and graciousness of the Old South with the marvels of the modern metropolis.

Alabama Bureau of Tourism and Travel, P.O. Box 4309, Montgomery, AL 36103-4308, 334-242-4169 or 800-ALABAMA.

Birmingham Convention and Visitors Bureau, 2200 Ninth Avenue North, Birmingham, AL 35203-1100, 205-252-9825 or 800-962-6453.

Montgomery Convention and Visitors Bureau, 401 Madison Avenue, Montgomery, AL 36104, 334-240-9452.

Selma–Dallas County Convention and Visitors Bureau, 513 Lauderdale Street, Selma, AL 36702, 334-875-7241.

Tuskegee Area Council on Tourism, P.O. Box 299, Tuskegee, AL 36083, 334-724-3786.

CHAPTER 5

THE COASTAL
CIRCLE TRAIL

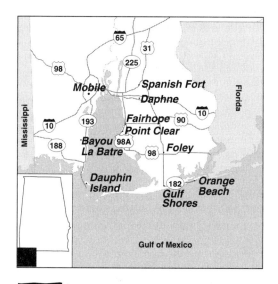

labama's Gulf Coast is a relatively undiscovered Eden of unspoiled beaches, picturesque small towns and fishing villages, glamorous historic Mobile, Civil War sites, copious blooming flowers and canopied avenues of live oaks, not to mention excellent fishing and fantastic seafood. Stretched in a huge horseshoe around Mobile Bay, this 155-mile trail can be explored by starting with Mobile at the top of the horseshoe. Whether you take the western side to Dauphin Island or the eastern route to Gulf Shores, you can complete a giant circle and avoid backtracking by crossing Mobile Bay on the Mobile Bay Ferry between Fort Gaines on Dauphin Island and Fort Morgan at Gulf Shores, which together anchor the horseshoe and guard the entrance to the bay. Allow at least three days for a complete tour, but preferably more.

Mobile, frequently called New Orleans in Miniature, shows off elaborate iron tracery gracing the balconies of both homes and commercial buildings. There are more than enough attractions to make Mobile a destination on its own. It is, after all, Alabama's second-largest city.

Steeped in history, Mobile has been under several flags during its three hundred-year history. The site was inhabited by Native Americans when Pierre Le Moyne d'Iberville and his brother, Jean Baptiste Le Moyne, Sieur de Bienville, Governor of Louisiana, claimed it for France in 1702, making it the first white settlement in Alabama and its capital until 1718. However, periods of English and Spanish rule followed, and Mobile became part of the United States in 1814. As the frontier was settled, Alabama became a leading producer of cotton. Mobile, as Alabama's only port, was the gateway to the world.

During the Civil War, Mobile was an important port for the Confederate States of America because it was through Mobile Bay that blockade runners were able to slip out to trade with the West Indies and Europe, keeping the southern cause alive. Mobile was one of the last ports to fall to Union forces, and the loss of Confederate battleships in Mobile Bay, followed by the fall of three nearby forts, resulted in the occupation of Mobile and eventually guaranteed victory for the Union in 1865. Economic recovery was slow in coming to Mobile after the war, but by the late 1800s shipbuilding had emerged as a major industry.

Mobile claims precedence over New Orleans in celebrating the first Mardi Gras in America in 1703—a hundred and twenty years before the tradition began in New Orleans—and the city still puts on quite a show each year. Simultaneous to Mardi Gras Day is the opening of the Azalea Trail Festival, during which you can drive or walk past 35 miles of some of the largest and most flamboyant azaleas in America. Visitors look forward to seeing the Azalea Trail Maids decked out in pastel antebellum gowns cascading with ruffles and accessorized with picture hats and parasols.

Whether you're a history buff or not, every tourist's first stop should be Fort Conde (150 South Royal Street, 334-434-7304), which serves as Mobile's Welcome Center. Reconstructed to its 1735 appearance, the fort features furniture, costumes, artillery, and artifacts from that era. Guards in French costumes daily demonstrate flintlock rifles and relate Mobile's history. Information about attractions, lodgings, and restaurants in the city is available.

Mobile is dedicated to the preservation of its historic buildings and districts. Four-thousand of the Preservation City's buildings are listed on the National Register of Historic Places. The historic preservation society has been active and influential since 1932 and has saved whole neighborhoods. Seven historic boundary districts have been identified. If you are doing a walking or driving tour, architecturally or historically significant buildings are identified by colorful shields. Maps for walking or driving tours of the neighborhoods are available at Fort Conde.

Many of these historical attractions are within walking distance of Fort Conde. Next door to the fort is the Conde-Charlotte Museum House (104 Theatre Street, 334-432-4722) operated by the Colonial Dames of America. Built in 1822 as the city's first jail, the house is considered to be one of the oldest structures in Mobile.

The centerpiece of the Oakleigh Historic District is the Oakleigh Period House Museum and Historic Complex (350 Oakleigh Place, 334-432-1281), the headquarters of the preservation society. Situated on three and a half landscaped acres, the complex includes Oakleigh itself, the Cox-Deasy House, the Minnie Mitchell Archives, and sunken gardens.

The antebellum Oakleigh house, built in 1833, was named for the three hundred and fifty oak trees on the property. Restored to its 1850 appearance, the mansion houses Civil War artifacts and Victorian,

Frilly ironwork adorns the porches and balconies in Mobile

Empire, and Regency antiques. Spared from plundering by Union soldiers, Oakleigh was a center of Mobile social life after the war.

The Richards DAR House (256 North Joachim Street, 334-434-
7320) on DeTonti Square is an Italianate antebellum townhouse
built by steamboat captain Charles G. Richards in the mid-1800s.
The square, straight building is famous for its lavish iron-lace trim
with neoclassical figurines of the Four Seasons adorning the iron
arabesques and scrolls and for the irreplaceable panes of red
Bohemian glass surrounding the front door. Plain and dull-looking
on the outside, the blood-red glass glows brilliantly and casts ever-
changing patterns on the walls and floors within. During the Civil
War both the Confederacy and then the Union used the house as
their naval headquarters.

Don't miss the 1855 Bragg-Mitchell Mansion (1906 Springhill
Avenue, 334-471-6364), which is Mobile's grandest antebellum
mansion. Built by Judge John Bragg, brother of Confederate General
Braxton Bragg, the combination Greek Revival and Italianate house
is surrounded by a grove of stately live oaks.

You can visit the Bragg-Mitchell mansion, Oakleigh, the Conde-
Charlotte House, and the Richards-DAR House with one general
admission ticket available at any of the four houses or by a telephone
order (334-471-6365).

The Museum of the City of Mobile (35 Government Street, 334-
434-7569) is housed in a restored 1872 townhouse with ornate iron
balconies. Documents, artifacts, antiques, early twentieth-century
costumes, riverboat and Civil War memorabilia, and a collection of
ornate horse-drawn carriages depict the history of Mobile. Of special
interest are elaborate coronation costumes of Mardi Gras queens
from the 1860s to the present—most of these outfits cost thousands
of dollars.

Dauphin Street has emerged as a hot location for nightspots and
eateries. Go to The Big Kahuna's Sports Cafe (273 Dauphin Street,
334-433-0500) for the best hamburger in town. Hayley's (278
Dauphin Street, 334-433-4970) has been voted "The Best Bar To
Hang Out In" for two years running. Grand Central (256 Dauphin

Street, 334-432-6999), is the place to see and be seen. Another popular spot is Port City Brewery (225 Dauphin Street, 334-438-2739),
Alabama's first micro-brewery (it also has a restaurant). Three
George's Candy (226 Dauphin Street, 334-433-6725) has been selling sweets to Mobilians and visitors since 1907. Watch them make
mouth-watering pralines, fudge, and divinity as well as chocolate cre-
ations to die for.

Mobile is rich in historic places to stay. The Radisson Admiral
Semmes Hotel (251 Government Street, 334-432-8000 or 800-333-
3333) is a restored, grand 1940s hotel retaining original architectural
features such as the marble rotunda while providing updated luxury
guest accommodations, and a restaurant, lounge, pool, and
whirlpool. Malaga Inn (359 Church Street, 334-438-4701 or 800-
235-1586), housed in two identical connected 1862 Spanish-style
townhouses, is magnificently furnished with antiques. The inn has a
pool, restaurant, and lounge.

Bed-and-breakfast accommodations can be found at Mallory
Manor (1104 Montauk Avenue, 334-432-6440), an 1874 home; or at
Stickney's Hollow (1604 Springhill Avenue, 334-456-4556 or 334-
432-1877), a lovely Victorian home nestled under ancient oaks
where a house has existed since 1805. In 1905 it was converted from
a Creole cottage to a Victorian townhouse. Complete apartments
are available.

Twenty miles southwest of Mobile off I-10, take US 90 south to
Theodore, site of Bellingrath Gardens and Home (12401
Bellingrath Gardens Road, 334-973-2217), which is one of the finest
private gardens in the country. Follow the signs to the gardens and
plan to spend at least a half day exploring the estate.

Magnificent in any season, the nine hundred acres on the Isle aux
Oies River showcase a sixty-five-acre landscaped garden and a
10,500-square-foot brick and wrought-iron mansion filled with an
extensive collection of antique furniture and priceless objets d'art,
including one of the world's largest collections of Boehm porcelains.
It's hard to imagine that local Coca-Cola bottling pioneer Walter

Bellingrath originally bought the property in 1918 for a fishing camp. After enjoying the property as a retreat with a few ramshackle buildings for several years, Mr. and Mrs. Bellingrath decided they wanted a new home in an Old World setting. They created the gardens with a combination of French, English, and Mediterranean influences and opened them to the public before they even began construction on the house. The house itself wasn't opened to the public until after Mr. Bellingrath's death in 1955.

Focal points of the gardens include a Victorian conservatory, a large Oriental-American garden, a bridal garden, a grotto with a spillway, and a bird sanctuary. Bellingrath Gardens is noted for cascading mums. In the fall you'll see masses of them dripping from every wall, bridge, and balcony or trained up forms to create tree shapes. Billed as a garden for all seasons, Bellingrath Gardens claims to have six seasons rather than four.

If you have a craving for fresh seafood while you are in the neighborhood, try Ellen's Place (14986 Dauphin Island Parkway, 334-873-4612). Just as famous for Black Angus beef, Ellen's specializes in surf-and-turf choices.

Take County 59 south to State 188 and turn west to **Bayou La Batre.** Once little known, the shrimping town is now basking in the celebrity it has earned from the movie *Forrest Gump* and its fictitious Bubba Gump Shrimp.

Although the area has been occupied at one time or another by the Spanish and the English and even by pirates, its citizens consider themselves French. In 1699 French explorers claimed the coast for the Sun King, Louis XIV. The town got its name from the remains of a French artillery battery located on the west bank of the bayou for defense.

Known for the quality of its fishing of all types, Bayou La Batre is considered the Seafood Capital of Alabama. The annual spring Blessing of the Fleet spotlights the significance of seafood to the community. Shrimpers and fishermen from a wide area of the coast sail into Bayou La Batre to ask God's blessing and protection for themselves and their boats and to pray for a bountiful harvest. The pageantry and beauty of the double-rigged shrimpers, neat white oyster boats, and little runabouts alive with flags and decorations and overflowing with family and friends bring thousands of visitors to watch boat owners compete for honors and prizes bestowed by the event's sponsor, Saint Margaret's Catholic Church. Activities include an official prayer, the dedication of a memorial wreath for lost fisherman, a boat parade, a golf tournament, a dance, an art show, an arts-and-crafts fair, fiddler-crab races, a pet show, rides for the youngsters, and, of course, a gigantic seafood feast featuring such delicacies as seafood-stuffed jalapenos, sharkburgers, fried squid, baked crabs, and seafood gumbo.

Saint Margaret's Catholic Church (State 188, 334-824-2415) is noted for the magnificent stained-glass windows brought from Ireland and Germany when the church was built in 1908. The windows memorialize the Daughters of Charity.

The greater Bayou La Batre region also encompasses Bayou Coteau, Bayou Coq d'Inde, and the tiny town of **Coden.** You can visit or drive by several stunning antebellum homes such as Royal Oaks and the Girard-Bosarge House.

It's not surprising that a combination of pirates and Civil War spies, murky, misty bayous, and tendrils of floating Spanish moss has given rise to several legends and ghost stories about the lady in white, the three white dogs, or Nasty Nancy and French Ellen.

Don't leave Bayou La Batre–Coden without sampling a delicious seafood meal. Try the Lighthouse (12495 Padgett Switch Road, 334-824-2500), Catalina's (State 188, 334-824-2104), or Mary's Place (5075 State 188, 334-873-4514). Plan to be in Bayou La Batre in October for the Taste of the Bayou festival.

Retrace your route on State 188 to State 193 and turn south to **Dauphin Island,** a relatively undiscovered Gulf Coast treasure. Cedar Point is the land's end just before you leave the mainland, and Cedar Point Fishing Pier (State 193, 334-873-4476) is a 1,200-foot-long lighted fishing pier.

Cross the 3-mile Dauphin Island Bridge on State 193 to the 15-mile-long island. Dauphin Island sports white quartz sand beaches that sometimes boast sand dunes as high as 35 feet. The island's atmosphere is unhurried and its beauty still pristine. It has not become overly commercialized, nor has it attracted high-rise hotels. In fact, condominiums and rental homes far outnumber hotels and motels. Roads cover only half of the island, and there are no traffic lights.

The French used the island—which is named for the son of Louis XIV—to anchor their colonization of the New World. Both the Spanish and British navies manned forts there before the Americans captured the island from the Spanish in 1813.

Dauphin Island was also strategically important during the Civil War. Together with Fort Morgan across Mobile Bay, Dauphin Island's Fort Gaines (Bienville Boulevard, 334-861-6992) protected the mouth of the bay and Mobile as well.

Established in 1821, the fort was originally a three-story structure, but during the brutal Civil War bombardment the top two stories were blown off.

The Battle of Mobile Bay was a devastating loss for the Confederacy. Fort Gaines, Fort Morgan, Fort Powell, and the Confederate fleet were unable to withstand three weeks of combined army and navy skirmishes and counterattacks by the Union.

The Battle of Mobile Bay is best remembered for Union Admiral D. G. Farragut's famous words "Damn the torpedoes! Full speed ahead!" Although eighteen Union ships lined up against the lonely ironclad CSS *Tennessee*, all was not smooth sailing for the Yankees. When the USS *Tecumseh* hit a mine (then known as a torpedo) and sank, other captains were afraid to go forward. It was then that Farragut uttered his famous words, and sheer numbers eventually prevailed. The CSS *Tennessee* finally surrendered when her smokestack was blown off and the ship was filled with smoke.

Today, the five-sided fort seems to echo with the sounds of Civil War battles. You can touch the actual cannons used during the conflict and tour the remaining buildings.

Artifacts at the Fort Gaines Museum trace various periods of history from the Native American through the English, colonial, American, Civil War, and Spanish/American eras up to the 1930s. Two absorbing exhibits are one looking at history from a women's perspective and one called *Voices from the Past*, which includes letters, cartoons, architectural plans, and other personal expressions of life at the fort.

Christmas at the Fort is a widely anticipated yearly event which recreates life at the fortress based on a letter written home by a Civil War soldier in 1861. Periodically, re-enactments of the Battle of Mobile Bay take place. Other events not to be missed are A Taste of the Fort (a food-tasting event) and the Haunted Fort nightly tours at Halloween. Storytellers are often on hand with tales of the past.

Adjacent to the fort is the hundred-and-fifty-site Fort Gaines Campground (334-861-2742), which offers free boat launches, a lighted boardwalk to a secluded beach, and walking trails that connect to the Audubon Bird Sanctuary.

Dauphin Island offers far more than history. Nature is at its best there. The island is a major bird migration flyway between South America and Canada, making it one of the premier birding spots in the Southeast. You can observe more than three hundred and forty species of birds at the hundred-and-sixty-acre Audubon Bird Sanctuary (334-861-2120). Another harbinger of spring is the first landfall made by monarch butterflies migrating north. Miles of nature walks in the sanctuary—some on boardwalks—give access to pine and live oak-forests, magnolia clearings, swampland, and beaches.

The fishing at Dauphin Island is some of the best in America. Excellent places to fish are the 850-foot-long Dauphin Island Fishing Pier and the East End Pier. Numerous charter boats take anglers out for deep-sea challenges. One of the benefits for residents and visitors is that you can buy fresh seafood right off the boats. Dauphin Island is the site of nine annual fishing rodeos, including the Alabama Deep Sea Fishing Rodeo. A full-service marina offers hookups and water for those fishing or traveling by boat.

With the easy access to fresh seafood, it's no wonder that restaurants such as Seafood Galley (1510 Bienville Boulevard, 334-861-

8000), Isle Dauphine Club (100 Orleans Avenue, 334-861-2433), and Barnacle Bill's (1518 Bienville Boulevard, 334-861-5255) abound. One store not to miss is Ship and Shore (401 Lemoyne Drive, 334-861-2262), a general store that claims "If we don't have it, we can get it for you tomorrow."

The premier annual event is the Dauphin Island Sail Boat Race. Held in the spring, it is the largest one-day sailing event in the country. Other special annual events include the Town of Dauphin Island Birthday and Spring Festival Weekend, which is scheduled to coincide with the return of the birds; the Battle of Mobile Bay re-enactment at Fort Gaines; and Christmas on the island featuring a parade, a pageant, a lighting competition, and a night-time boat parade.

To reach **Fort Morgan** on the opposite side of the bay and the beaches beyond, take the scenic thirty-minute ferry ride aboard the auto/passenger Mobile Bay Ferry (334-421-6420 or 800-634-4027), which has frequent daily departures from both sides of the bay. The ferry started service in 1979 after Hurricane Frederic destroyed the old drawbridge. The ferry provided the only means of transport on and off Dauphin Island for three years until the existing bridge was built. Once the bridge was rebuilt, the ferry resumed its route across the bay. Occasionally the ferry has to suspend service because of high seas, in which case you'll have to drive the 100 miles all the way around the bay.

Fort Morgan (Mobile Point, 334-540-7125), built between 1819 and 1834, guards the main shipping channel into Mobile Bay. The fort was occupied by Confederate troops for most of the Civil War. Following the Battle of Mobile Bay, Fort Morgan was subjected to a four-day siege that ended with a twenty-four-hour bombardment. It was able to hold out longer than Fort Gaines and didn't surrender until August 23, 1864.

After the Civil War the fortress was unused until 1898, just before the outbreak of the Spanish-American War. It was during that time that the fortification was modernized with concrete bastions. Fort Morgan remained active until 1923. During World War I it was used as a training base for artillery troops preparing to go overseas and was one

Spinnakers fill for a run down Mobile Bay

of the first schools for training anti-aircraft gunners. Abandoned again, the fortification was reactivated during World War II, after which it was donated to the state of Alabama for use as a historical park.

The museum exhibits chronicle the history of Fort Morgan. There's also a lighthouse exhibit and an exhibit from the 1906 hurricane, the most destructive hurricane the area has ever seen.

You can find bed-and-breakfast accommodations nearby at The Square Flower (7013 Seashell Drive, 334-540-7279), located on the gulf side of Fort Morgan. Its quiet, secluded atmosphere is ideal for beach lovers.

From Fort Morgan a short ride east on State 180 will take you to **Gulf Shores, Orange Beach,** and **Perdido Key.** Commonly known as Alabama's Gulf Coast, this area is also affectionately dubbed the Redneck Riviera. Located 50 miles southeast of Mobile and 35 miles west of Pensacola, Florida, Alabama's Gulf Coast is bordered on the south by the Gulf of Mexico, on the east by Perdido Bay, on the north by the Intracoastal Waterway, and on the west by Mobile Bay. The thirty-thousand-acre island has 32 miles of white sand beaches. Freshwater lakes, rivers, bayous, and coves add nearly four hundred thousand acres of protected waterfront to the area.

Like most beach areas, Alabama's Gulf Coast offers a variety of activities. There are four championship golf courses and fourteen public tennis courts in addition to the courts at many hotels. Freshwater and saltwater fishing, scuba diving, snorkeling, parasailing, and boat rentals round out the watersports. Other attractions include a water park, miniature golf, hot-air ballooning, and a zoo. One of our favorite activities has always been horseback riding on the beach, although there are fewer and fewer places where you can still do that. However, Horseback Beach Rides, Inc. (State 180 near Fort Morgan, 334-943-6674) offers a one-hour beach ride and a one-hour country trail ride.

Locals recommend the following Gulf Shores restaurants and night spots: the Pink Pony Pub (137 East Gulf Place, 334-948-6731); Shirley & Wayne's Supper Club (25125 Perdido Beach Boulevard, 334-981-4818), popular among retirees for dinner and dancing; and Floribama (17401 Perdido Key Drive, 334-981-8555). Located on the Florida-Alabama border, Floribama features such activities as a Mullet Toss. With three to four live bands each weekend and visits from such notables as football's Kenny Stabler, Floribama is popular with everyone from bikers to preppies. Sea-N-Suds Restaurant and Oyster Bar (405 East Beach Road, 334-948-7894) is located on the pier overlooking the Gulf. Perched high above the Gulf Shores Surf and Racquet Club on West Beach Boulevard, The View Restaurant (334-

948-8888) offers a spectacular gulf view and unsurpassed cuisine.

Gulf Shores offers a wide variety of accommodations—everything from large hotel resorts to small motels to condominiums to cottages to camping. Between Gulf Shores and Orange Beach is Gulf State Park (21250 East Beach Boulevard, 334-948-4853 or 800-544-4853), which offers 2.5 miles of beachfront, an eighteen-hole golf course, and lighted tennis courts, as well as six thousand acres of protected wilderness that includes three hundred acres covered by nature trails and two freshwater lakes. Accommodations range from a 144-room beachside hotel to modern and rustic cabins to a 468-site campground. The Sand Castle Dining Room specializes in all-you-can-eat buffets for breakfast and dinner. To contact the hotel call 334-948-4853 or 800-544-4853; for cabin information call 334-948-7275; or for campground details call 334-948-6353.

Continue on State 180 to Orange Beach and Perdido Key, an area which is less congested than Gulf Shores. Perdido Key links Florida to Orange Beach and is known for back bays, gulf views, and riverfront dockage. Condominiums make up the majority of accommodations. Perdido Key Resort (27200 Perdido Beach Boulevard, 334-981-9811) is a shell-pink Mediterranean-style palace rated with four diamonds by AAA. Ono Island is an exclusive enclave with some luxury rentals. Another choice is The Original Romar House, a seaside bed-and-breakfast (23500 Perdido Beach Boulevard, 334-981-6156 or 800-48-ROMAR). Located in a 1924 house, this bed and breakfast offers six rooms, a sumptuous southern breakfast, afternoon wine and cheese in The Purple Parrot Bar, a two-seater bicycle to borrow, and a hot tub.

As the home port for Alabama's famous deep-sea fishing fleet, Orange Beach offers a wide variety of seafood restaurants: Live Bait Food and Spirits (24281 Perdido Beach Boulevard, 334-981-6677); Tacky Jack's (Cotton Bayou Marina, 334-981-4144) for a hearty breakfast or dinner; Miss Kitty's (12408 South Seventh Street, 334-962-2701) for great cheeseburgers; Hemingway's (27075 Marina Road in Orange Beach Marina, 334-981-9791) for seafood and Cajun specialties such as Eggplant Pirogue; Nolan's (East Beach Boulevard, 334-948-2111); and Voyagers at the Perdido Beach

Resort (27200 Perdido Beach Boulevard, 334-981-9811), which is the only AAA Four Diamond restaurant in Alabama and serves Gulf Coast Creole cuisine.

From Orange Beach return to Gulf Shores on State 180 and turn north on State 59 to **Foley.** The historic downtown area is filled with small boutiques, bookshops, unique eateries, and an old-fashioned soda fountain. The Foley Art Center (119 West Laurel Avenue, 334-4381) and the Performing Arts Association are housed in the seventy-seven-year-old Foley Hotel. Artworks by local artists are for sale.

However, Foley is essentially a commercial area with miniature golf, an amusement and water park, a zoo, several antique malls, and the Riviera Center outlet mall.

East of town on US 98 in **Elberta** is the Baldwin Heritage Museum (334-966-8375), a farm museum. Baldwin County is one of the richest agricultural regions in the nation and is inhabited by as many different ethnic and national backgrounds as any other county in the South. The museum, which resembles a turn-of-the-century barn with a typical working windmill, displays documents and photographs, farm machinery and vehicles, tools, household and mercantile furnishings, clothing, and other objects relating to the county's history. The original Saint Mark's Lutheran Church has been moved to the grounds and plans call for construction of a small crossroads community of relocated historic buildings.

From Foley go west on US 98 to **Magnolia Springs,** where you will find the Inspiration Oak. This ancient tree—more than five hundred years old—gained national attention in 1990 when it was attacked and poisoned by a person or persons unknown. Despite heroic efforts by noted tree surgeons, the tree has died. Visitors still come to see it, and plans are underway to preserve it.

Weeks Bay National Estuarine Research Reserve (US 98, 334-928-9792) protects three thousand acres of wetlands. On the nature trail you can explore four different types of habitats.

Pass US 98 and take Scenic 98 north to **Point Clear,** originally named Punta Clara by the Spanish. Since the turn of the century Point Clear has been a summer sanctuary for members of Mobile society. In 1890 a score of 198-by-1,000-foot lots were sold and lavish Victorian summer homes and a long boardwalk fronting on the bay were built. Descendants of many of the original families still summer in these cottages.

When we visited with a family of long-time residents, we learned the ins and outs of life at Point Clear. For example, while admiring the lengthy docks, some with gazebos, we were corrected, "We don't call them docks, they're wharves." Scenic State 98 is known as the Back Road and talking about someone is referred to as "palavering over them." The extra overhangs on the enormous verandas are rain porches, built out beyond the porch roofs so that residents can enjoy the outdoors even in bad weather.

Even before the summer homes were built Point Clear was a resort area. The Grand Hotel (Scenic US 98, 334-928-9201 or 800-544-9933) was built in 1847. During the Civil War it served as a hospital. On the hotel grounds is Confederate Rest, a cemetery where three hundred Confederate soldiers are buried.

The present hotel (a Marriott) at the secluded bayfront resort was built in 1941 amid five hundred and fifty acres of moss-draped grounds. If you're lucky, you'll be greeted at the door by Bucky Miller. Employed the first day in 1941, he's still on the job and will be more than happy to regale you with tales of the hotel and might even share his recipe for hot mint toddy.

Thirty-six holes of golf, tennis, watersports, a supervised Children's Fun Camp, and more are offered at the Grand Hotel.

While you are in the Point Clear area, a great place to eat delicious seafood meals is the Pelican Pointe Grill (10299 County 1, 334-928-1747 or 334-928-4414). The best bet is their combo platters.

Miss Colleen's House (Scenic Highway 98, 334-928-8477) is a delicious attraction in more ways than one. The sprawling Victorian house, built in 1897 by Edward Brodbeck (Miss Colleen's father), features several rooms of Victorian antiques, all from the family. Located in the old dining room is the Punta Clara Kitchen, owned and operated by Dorothy Brodbeck Pacey and family. What began as a hobby has turned into a major candy-making operation. Punta Clara Kitchen is famous for its cakes, cookbooks, jams, jellies, relishes, and ice-cream toppings such as bourbon and brandy, chocolate pecan, or rum praline. Punta Klara Kitchen also has a variety of sugar-free items.

The Wash House restaurant is located in an old building at the rear of the property, which backs onto Mobile Bay. Miss Colleen's is located 1.5 miles from the Grand Hotel and can be reached on foot by way of the boardwalk. Stop by, call, or write for a catalog of Punta Clara Kitchen specialties.

Continuing north of Point Clear on Scenic US 98, you'll come to **Fairhope.** Begun in 1894 as a tax colony where there would be no private ownership of land, the community was a potential utopia, which enthusiasts thought had a "fair hope of succeeding." Today, only the waterfront and a small park in Fairhope are still owned by the tax colony and won't ever be developed.

Fairhope is in the fastest-growing county in Alabama. The quaint Carmel-like downtown, centered on Fairhope and Section Streets and extending several blocks, is beautifully landscaped and filled with upscale specialty shops and boutiques.

Near the center of town you may see a local character—the Tomato Lady. For years and in all kinds of weather she's been on the street corner selling tomatoes off the back of her pickup truck. Some local citizens thought it would be nice to give her an empty storefront out of which to operate. Before they knew it, she was back on the street corner. When asked why, she replied, "I wanted to see and talk to people."

The Montrose Historic District is located in an area originally known as Ecor Rouge or Red Bluff, which is the highest point on the coastline between Maine and Mexico. Drive by the numerous historic homes.

Recommended places to eat include Marianne's Deli (7 South Church Street, 334-928-3663) and Jus Gumbo (2 South Church Street, 334-928-4100), known for its fabulous po' boy sandwiches.

Fairhope offers a wealth of bed and breakfasts from which to choose.

Bay Breeze Guest House (742 South Mobile Street, 334-928-8976) on Mobile Bay has its own pier and beach; Church Street Inn (515 South Church Street, 334-928-8976) is an antique-filled home built in the 1920s; The Guest House (63 South Church Street, 334-928-6226) is in a historic Victorian house within walking distance of the bay; and Marcella's Tea Room and Inn (114 Fairhope Avenue, 334-990-8520) offers bed-and-breakfast accommodations in the main house and a cottage, as well as providing a tea room for private functions.

North of Fairhope, Scenic 98 merges with US 98, which you take to get to **Daphne,** best known for Jubilee—an incredible and largely unexplained natural phenomenon that occurs only within a twenty-mile area. For some strange reason, all types of sealife come to the surface at the same time in a place where they can be easily caught. Imagine scooping up armloads of shrimp, lobsters, or other sea creatures with little effort. Jubilee is most likely to occur between May and September and between midnight and dawn one or more times in a summer. Folks take turns patrolling the beaches during the night. If you see the phenomenon beginning, it is your duty to let everyone else know. Folks come out with gigs, washtubs, nets, or anything else with which to scoop up and carry home the bounty of the sea. Bonfires are lit and Jubilee becomes a big beach party.

It is speculated that Jubilee may be caused by quick changes in the amount of fresh water meeting salt water (such as after a heavy rain), which changes the oxygen level and forces sea life to the surface. On the other hand, the phenomenon may have something to do with the position of the moon.

Daphne is the home of the American Sport Art Museum and Archives (One Academy Drive, 334-626-3303), a museum dedicated to the preservation of sports history, art, and literature. In addition to displays of the works of internationally famous artists, the museum has an outstanding collection of Olympic posters.

Leave Daphne on US 98 going north and turn east on State 59 to **Malbis,** named for Jason Malbis, a Greek monk who came to America in 1907 to establish a religious refuge where there would be no private possession of property or money. Between 1960 and 1965, the remaining fifty members of the community planned and paid one million dollars for the magnificent Byzantine-style Malbis Greek Orthodox Cathedral (29300 County 27, 334-626-3050).

An exact copy of a church in Athens, Greece, the Malbis cathedral features marble from the same quarry that provided marble for the Parthenon. Mosaics adorn the exterior. Three master painters from Greece spent eight months on the interior embellishments. The interior is so colorful that it has been described as stepping into a rainbow.

Take State 225 north from Malbis to Historic Blakely State Park (33707 State 225, 334-626-0798), which is located on a significant Civil War battlefield. The extensive breastworks at the thirty-eight-hundred-acre park stretch 5.5 miles and are considered among the best preserved in the country. Also surviving are earthen forts, redoubts, rifle pits, and battery sites. Blakely is the largest site east of the Mississippi River to be listed on the National Register of Historic Places.

The Battle of Blakely was fought on April 9, 1865—the same day that General Robert E. Lee surrendered at Appomattox—and is considered to be the last major battle of the Civil War.

Nature trails, a quarter mile of waterfront boardwalk with two observation decks on the Tensaw River, 10.5 miles of riding and bicycle trails, three fishing ponds, and numerous camp sites enable visitors to explore the forest and riverbanks.

Visit the park during one of its special events. Fall brings the Blakely Country Music Blast, a two-day event featuring Nashville, Cajun, and bluegrass music. The Fort Blakely Battle Festival, which includes a re-enactment, is held the weekend closest to April 9.

Retrace your route to **Spanish Fort.** At the USS *Alabama* Battleship Memorial Park (Battleship Parkway, 334-433-2703) you can explore the decommissioned battleship, which was built in 1942. The ship played a prominent role in World War II, first serving with the British Royal Navy protecting convoys supplying Russia and then protecting aircraft carriers in the Pacific. A self-contained city, the USS *Alabama* has an operating room, sick bay, dental office, blacksmith and metalsmith shop, darkroom and printing shop, laundry,

Come aboard the USS *Alabama*, a battleship which served in both
the Atlantic and Pacific in World War II

cobbler shop, barber shop, tailor shop, soda fountain, and brig.

You can also tour the submarine USS *Drum* and see a replica of
the CSS *Hundley*, an eight-man Civil War submarine operated by
crankshaft. The *Hundley* was the first submarine developed by either
navy. It was made of iron and could sneak up on other ships as

though it had supernatural powers, giving it the name Iron Witch. Also located in the hundred-acre park are several historic aircraft: a B-52 bomber, several World War II fighter planes, and a Redstone rocket. Other attractions include seventeen hundred varieties of roses, a nature observatory, and a gazebo.

Take an afternoon or dinner-entertainment cruise around Mobile Bay aboard the *Commander*, which is docked in Battleship Park (334-433-6101). The captain entertains with stories about Civil War naval battles as well as pointing out Sand Island and the huge ships, oil rigs, and dry-dock facilities in Mobile harbor.

In few areas of the state are so much history and so many attractions packed into such a small, compact area—most of which is covered by water—making Mobile Bay and the Gulf Coast a vacation paradise.

Alabama Gulf Coast Chamber of Commerce/Convention and Visitors Bureau, State 59 South, P.O. Drawer 457, Gulf Shores, AL 36542, 334-968-7511.

Baldwin Welcome Center, I-10 west of Florida state line, P.O. Box 699, Robertsdale, AL 36567, 334-946-3375.

South Baldwin Chamber of Commerce, State 59 and State 98, P.O. Box 1117, Foley, AL 36536, 334-943-3291.

Bayou La Batre Chamber of Commerce, North Wintzell Avenue, Bayou La Batre, AL 36509, 334-824-4088.

Town of Dauphin Island, P.O. Box 610, Dauphin Island, AL 36528, 334-861-5524.

Dauphin Island Park and Beach Board, P.O. Box 97, Dauphin Island, AL 36528, 334-861-3607.

Eastern Shore Chamber of Commerce, 327 Fairhope Avenue, Fairhope, AL 36532, 334-928-6387.

Grand Bay Welcome Center, I-10 east of Mississippi state line, P.O. Drawer 626, Grand Bay, AL 36541, 334-865-4741.

Orange Beach Chamber of Commerce, State 182, Orange Beach, AL 36561, 334-981-8859.

CHAPTER 6

FIELDS OF GREEN: ROBERT TRENT JONES GOLF TRAIL

In a real-life instance of "If you build it, they will come," Retirement Systems of Alabama (RSA) has created an exciting new concept in golf courses: seven challenging upscale public facilities with a total of eighteen courses and 324 holes. Named for its creator, golfing great and course designer extraordinaire Robert Trent Jones Sr., who is one of only two course

designers in the World Golf Hall of Fame, the magnificent achieve-
ment of the 342-mile Robert Trent Jones Golf Trail has catapulted
Alabama, practically overnight, into the top ten golf destinations in
this country as ranked by the National Golf Foundation.

Alabama had long languished at the bottom of the heap when it
came to American golf—forty-eighth out of the fifty states. In fact,
Alabama was considered to be merely a pass-through state by thousands of winter golfers bound for Florida. However, in an epiphanous
moment of foresight, Dr. David Bonner, CEO of the RSA, saw a single way to attract retirees, tourists, and industries to Alabama: a series
of magnificent public golf courses.

Traditionally, public golf has meant hard, uneven greens, bald fairways, and primitive clubhouses. The challenge was to create facilities
in the style of luxurious country clubs with well-maintained championship courses and upscale clubhouses.

Among the state's older courses are several designed by Robert
Trent Jones Sr., the most prolific and innovative golf architect of all
time, who designed five hundred courses worldwide, of which thirty-
five are on Golf Digest's list of "America's 100 Greatest Golf
Courses." Naturally Jones was approached to design this boldly ambi-
tious venture, which is the largest golf course construction project
ever attempted anywhere. Jones described the trail as "one of the
greatest achievements of my life and probably the most magnificent
courses I've ever designed. This land was some of the best property
I've ever worked with. When you start with great land, you end up
with great golf courses."

Strategically located throughout the state, the courses are anything but cookie-cutter layouts. They offer golfers the experience of
all types of topography, scenery, and vegetation. Stretching the
entire length of the state from mountainous Huntsville to Mobile on
the Gulf of Mexico, the facilities are no more than fifteen minutes
off an interstate and no more than two hours from each other. In
addition, they are located close to cities or towns with a wide variety
of attractions and comfortable accommodations. Golfers can make a
week's vacation out of playing one course at each facility. It would

take two to three weeks to play all the courses once. Total par on all the courses is 1,089.

The bold plan and the singular beauty and extraordinary inherent character of each site on the trail has transformed Alabama's landscape, as well as the overall impression of the state, while establishing an exhilarating gauge for the game itself.

Although their layouts are vastly different, the courses have much in common. Each is designed for tournament and individual play. Multiple-tee placements—often as many as seven to eleven per hole—permit golfers to play from their own skill levels. The tee boxes are scattered so that golfers may never play a hole the same way twice. Par-three short courses are regulation courses with water hazards, sand bunkers, and large tiered greens, but with only half the distance, averaging 3,400–3,600 yards.

The amenities at each club are similar. Spacious, well-appointed clubhouses are encircled by vast southern plantation-style verandas furnished with heavy rockers. Inside, each is decorated with displays of antique golf memorabilia, plush carpets, and substantial, comfortable furniture. Each offers a full-service pro shop, a snack bar, dining facilities, locker rooms, and conference space.

All courses feature low greens fees and cart fees that remain uniform year round. Indulge your passion for golf with a Robert Trent Jones Trail Pass or Trail Sampler. The Trail Pass comes in three-, five-, and seven-day increments and entitles the golfer to unlimited greens fees at any of the facilities with no restrictions on days or times that the pass may be used. The Trail Sampler entitles the bearer to one greens fee per course at each facility, again with no restrictions on days or times. Inclusive group outing packages are also available.

The RTJ Golf Trail Automated Tee Time Reservation System offers a quick, easy way to reserve tee time twenty-four hours a day, seven days a week. You may use the automated system to reserve a tee time up to three days in advance, but not for same-day reservations. Using a touch-tone phone, dial the number of the facility at which you wish to play and follow the instructions. Have a credit card handy.

Tee off on the Robert Trent Jones Golf Trail

Jones once said that "God builds golf courses. Men just go out and find them." You'll want to go out and find the new courses on the RTJ Golf Trail.

The courses are listed below:

The northern part of the state boasts three of the courses on the trail. Huntsville's Hampton Cove (4850 Old US 431S, Owens Cross Road, 35763, 205-551-1818), southeast of town, offers fifty-four holes on three distinctly different courses that include two championship courses and an eighteen-hole short course covering six hundred and fifty acres. The Highland Course has a Scottish-style layout set against a mountain panorama. The bunker-free River Course, which follows the Flint River, uses only natural grass traps. It is the only course of its kind anywhere.

In Birmingham, Oxmoor Valley (100 Sunbelt Parkway, 35211, 205-942-1177) consists of two regulation eighteen-hole courses and an eighteen-hole short course on 600 acres of the peaks and valleys of the Appalachian foothills. The Ridge Course, which follows roller-coaster fairways, has the most severe terrain of all the courses on the trail. The entire Valley Course stretches two miles downrange with its first tee playing all the way down Little Shades Mountain. To reach the course, take the Lakeshore Parkway Exit W off I-65, go 1.5 miles and turn left on West Oxmoor Road; then go 3.5 miles to where it becomes Shannon-Oxmoor Road.

Gadsden's Silver Lakes (1 Sunbelt Parkway, 35905, 205-892-3268), situated on scenic rolling terrain next to the Talladega National Forest, offers three championship nine-hole courses and a nine-hole short course. This breathtaking location features a waterfall, hardwood and pine forests, and spectacular hilltop views. Seven of the nine holes on the short course are played over Lee's Lake. Take the I-759 exit from I-59, then US 431 to Glencoe.

In the central part of the state in Auburn-Opelika (3000 Sunbelt Parkway, Opelika, 36801, 334-749-9042), the Grand National—which Jones himself describes as "the most spectacular golf site in the world"—is built in a dramatic setting around six-hundred-acre Lake Saugahatchee and offers two eighteen-hole championship courses plus an eighteen-hole short course. Its award-winning Links Course was named the "Second-Best New Public Course" by *Golf Digest*, and its Lakes Course was named the "Fourth-Best" in 1993.

Thirty-two holes border water, and there is even an island green. From I-85 exit onto US 280, then go north on Lee County 97.

There are three courses in the southern part of the state. Highland Oaks in Dothan (904 Royal Parkway, 36301, 334-712-2820) features three nine-hole courses and a nine-hole short course all set amidst gentle rolling terrain with creeks, lakes, trees, marshes, and wetlands. The Marshwood Nine includes a 701-yard hole, the longest on the trail. To reach the course take US 231 to US 84.

Breathtaking is a word that is often over-used, but it is true of Greenville's stunning Cambrian Ridge course (1591 Braggs Road, 36037, 334-382-9787), where the terrain has more elevation changes than any other trail facility. From the clubhouse perched on the highest point in the region you'll get a striking view of nearly thirty miles. The thirty-six holes include three nine-hole courses and a nine-hole short course. The first hole on the Canyon Course drops 250 feet from the tee to the landing area, and hole three on the Sterling Course drops 300 feet. Take exit 130 from I-65 and go west on State 185 to State 263 to County 44; then turn left and go to a stop sign. Turn right into the entrance to the course.

In Mobile, Magnolia Grove (7000 Lamplighter Drive, Semmes, 36575; mailing address is P.O. Box 180305, Mobile, 36618, 334-645-0075) features the eighteen-hole Falls Course, the eighteen-hole Crossings Course (so named because it crosses railroad tracks twice), and an eighteen-hole short course. The thirteen hundred acres are noted for their wetlands, creeks, marshes, pine woods, and abundant wildlife. The Falls Course features a waterfall flowing down long steps at the tenth green, and the Crossings Course is noted for the Terminator, its killer finishing hole. From I-65 take Exit 5B onto US 98 to Schillinger Road, then turn left to the clubhouse.

You can get information on all these courses by calling Sun-Belt Golf Corporation (800-949-4444) or by contacting the individual course.

Alabama has many other golf courses that are open to public play or that have reciprocal arrangements with various country clubs around the country. For more information, consult the following golf publications: *Fairways,* the Gulf Coast Golf Guide, available at many visitors centers, and *Golf Alabama,* available from the Alabama Bureau of Tourism and Travel.

CHAPTER 7

HOT WHEELS
TO ROLL
TIDE TRAIL:
TALLADEGA TO
TUSCALOOSA

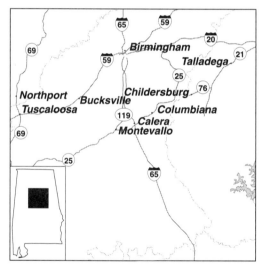

F rom the hot wheels of the world's fastest racetrack to the Crimson Tide of the University of Alabama, the Hot Wheels to Roll Tide Trail rambles 195 miles through central Alabama—an area not only diverse in topography, but also in its history, its towns, and its people. The trail offers a feast of attractions including architectural gems from the antebellum and Victorian periods, museums, black heritage sites, a winery, Alabama's highest peak, onyx and marble caverns, an extensive collection of Washingtonia, ancient Indian mounds, and huge ironworks furnaces.

Begin in **Talladega**—located about 10 miles south of I-20 in east-central Alabama between Anniston and Birmingham—a town best known for fast and furious motor racing. The world's fastest speedway, the Talladega Superspeedway (3366 Speedway Boulevard, 205-362-2261), draws fans to the heart-pounding excitement of two annual NASCAR Winston Cup events. The Winston 500 is held the first Sunday in May and the DieHard 500 in late July. There are support races on Saturdays prior to the two Sunday events.

Talladega holds the record for the fastest 500-mile race—186.288 mph—and the fastest pole-qualifying speed—212.809 mph. The inaugural NASCAR Busch Series race held at Talladega in 1992 set a record for the highest average speed of a race—158.359 mph.

In addition to paintings and awards honoring the inductees to the International Motorsports Hall of Fame and Museum (Speedway Boulevard, 205-362-5002), more than one hundred racing vehicles and racing memorabilia from 1902 to the present are also exhibited.

The Annual Induction Ceremony, which is open to the public, has been named one of the Top 20 Events in the Southeast by the Southeast Tourism Society. Another popular annual event is the Budweiser International Motorsports Expo Checkered Flag Weekend. Racing personalities are on hand and exhibits feature apparel and collectibles, racing parts and services, and Legends Cars Demonstration Events.

The complex features five other halls of fame: the Alabama Sports Writers Hall of Fame, the ARCA Hall of National Champions, the Western Auto Mechanics Hall of Fame, the Quarter Midgets of America Hall of Fame, and the World Karting Hall of Fame.

In downtown Talladega is the Talladega-Texaco Walk of Fame and Davey Allison Memorial, which honors Alabama notables in racing history. The walking track and park, dedicated in July 1994, are constructed as a tri-oval just like the Talladega Superspeedway. At pit row is a marble monument to racing superstar Davey Allison, who died in a helicopter crash at the racetrack. Marble markers bearing the Texaco star and the likenesses, names, and signatures of racing's original Alabama Gang (Donnie and Bobby Allison, Red Farmer, and Neil Bonnett) are placed around the track.

Talladega Short Track (Speedway Boulevard across from the Superspeedway, 205-831-1413), one of the South's most competitive clay ovals, features six racing divisions with races held every Saturday evening from March through October. Midget and go-cart races are held on Friday nights.

Despite Talladega's present and futuristic orientation, the city has a rich historical past. The Indian village of Talladega was located at the site of Big Spring. The site of the spring is marked by the Big Spring Monument (Battle and Spring Streets, one block west of the square).

Although cotton plantations brought prosperity to the area, citizens were divided about seceding from the Union; in fact, all three delegates from Talladega County voted against secession. After the Civil War, cotton mills and railroads brought prosperity back to Talladega.

The Silk Stocking District, a hundred-and-thirteen-acre area south of the courthouse square, was the enclave of leading merchants, lawyers, doctors, and local officials around the turn of the century. The wives of these wealthy citizens were the only ladies in town who could afford to wear silk stockings, hence the name. Encompassing the finest concentration of late-nineteenth-century and early-twentieth-century homes in Talladega, the structures in this district range from simple, unadorned cottages to elaborate Queen Anne and Eastlake houses.

Get an audiotape and a brochure that describe the seventy-five houses included in "A Tour of Talladega's Silk Stocking District" from the Greater Talladega Area Chamber of Commerce, located in the 1906 Louisville and Nashville Railroad Depot (210 East Street South, 205-362-9075).

Heritage Hall (200 South Street East, 205-761-1364), located in the heart of the Silk Stocking District, was built in 1908 to house the Jemison-Carnegie Library. Today, it is the repository of the Talladega and Alabama Heritage historic photograph collection—a tapestry revealing the lush, diverse history of east-central Alabama.

Other historic districts include the Talladega College Campus District, the Courthouse Square District, and the Boxwood Historic Complex.

Talladega College, Alabama's oldest private, black four-year liberal arts college, was established by freedmen in 1867. The beautiful campus boasts several landmark buildings: Swayne Hall, the earliest building; the President's home; DeForest Chapel; and Savery Library, which houses the historically significant Amistad murals by Hale Woodruff. These murals depict the successful quest for freedom by captured Africans aboard the slave ship *The Amistad*.

Talladega has the second-largest population of hearing-impaired citizens in the country. Restored buildings at the Alabama Institute for the Deaf and Blind (205 East South Street, 205-761-3206) include Manning Hall, constructed by slaves in the 1850s; William F. Grace Hall, built in 1878; and Jemison House, built in 1898.

During the three-day event called April in Talladega, historic homes are open for tours. Other attractions include an antique sale, box lunches, a tearoom, and museum exhibits.

Outside of town is Bryant Vineyard (1454 Griffitt Bend Road, 205-268-2638), a small, family-owned farm winery producing champagne and premium table wines from estate-grown scuppernongs, muscadines, and French hybrid grapes. Open Thursday through Saturday, the winery offers tours, tastings, and wine sales.

The Talladega area boasts several historic bed and breakfasts. Somerset House Bed and Breakfast (701 North Street, 205-761-9251 or 800-701-6678) is in a turn-of-the-century house. Historic Oakwood Bed and Breakfast (715 East North Street, 205-362-0662) is one of the finest examples of Federal architecture in Alabama.

From the country setting of Orangevale Plantation (1400 Whiting Road, 205-362-3052), you can see the depression in the ground that was the Jackson Trace. Accommodations are available in the 1852 Greek Revival mansion, in an 1830s Talladega County homestead cabin, in the old kitchen, or in the double-pen log cabin.

The Governor's House (500 Meadowlake Lane, 205-763-2186) was built in 1850 by former Alabama governor Lewis Parsons. Relocated to Meadowlake Farm, it is filled with antiques.

From Talladega take State 21 south and turn west on State 76 to DeSoto Caverns (5181 DeSoto Caverns Parkway, 205-378-7252 or 800-933-CAVE) east of **Childersburg.** DeSoto Caverns is one of the premier natural wonders in the southeast. The historic onyx and marble caves, formed out of dolomites and dolomitic limestones during the Cambrian-Ordovician age, were named for the Spanish explorer who passed through the area in 1540.

The main room—the Great Onyx Cathedral, which is larger than a football field and higher than a twelve-story building—holds one of the most concentrated accumulations of onyx-marble stalagmites and stalactites found in America. While you admire the strange formations such as soda straws, columns, popcorn or cave coral, draperies, flowstones, helictites, and rimstone dams and terraces, keep in mind that it takes an average of two hundred years for a formation to grow one cubic inch. The Onyx Draperies are among the largest free-hanging rock formations in the world, extending over thirty feet in length.

DeSoto Caverns has a constant year-round temperature of sixty degrees. However, nearly one hundred percent humidity makes the air seem close to normal room temperature. Amazingly enough, plant life grows in the caves, although the plants are not green, and some insects and other animal life have adapted to survive in a dark environment.

Traders Rock, with an inscription carved on it in 1723, proves that the cave was used as a shelter by early traders. The caverns were one of the first officially recorded caves in this country when they were rediscovered in 1796. During Prohibition, DeSoto Caverns became a speakeasy and square-dance hall. Arguments led to so many gunfights that it became known as The Bloody Bucket. Scenes from three movies have been filmed in the caverns: *Rascals & Robbers: The Further Adventures of Tom Sawyer & Huckleberry Finn, Jaws of Satan,* and *The Lost Platoon.*

An hour-long tour describes the history and formation of the caves and includes a laser light and sound show with leaping waters. In addition to the underground formations, you can see a prehistoric Indian burial ground over two thousand years old and a Confederate gunpowder mining center with the original well and leaching trench, and a reconstructed vat operation. You can also pan for gold or gemstones. The park contains a maze, playground, gift shop, and campground.

Annual events include the Indian Dance and Crafts Festival held in April; an Easter sound, laser light, and water show; the Antique Car and Music Show held in June; Coosa Fest in July, celebrating the Coosa Indians; September Fest, which includes a Civil War re-enactment; and Christmas at DeSoto Caverns, which also features a sound, laser light, and water show. Groups can pre-arrange an overnight experience in the caves at any time of the year.

Farther along State 76 is Childersburg, which claims to be the oldest city in America. In 1540, after De Soto met the Coosa Indians, he left behind a small group of Spanish people and one black, thereby establishing the claim to continuous occupancy and confirming Old Cosa, now Childersburg, as the oldest city in the country. A De Soto Monument commemorates the explorer's visit.

Take County 46 off State 76 to the Kymulga Grist Mill (County 46/36, 205-378-7436), where corn is still ground. Built by slaves in 1864, it is one of Alabama's oldest mills. It contains five sets of grinding stones, two of which came from France. One of five mills under construction at the outbreak of the Civil War, it was the only one to escape burning by Union troops. Also on the grounds is the Kymulga covered bridge over Talladega Creek, the largest cluster of white oak trees east of the Mississippi, the largest sugarberry tree in Alabama, two miles of nature trails, and the Burton Country Store.

Return to State 76 and continue west to **Columbiana,** where the second-largest collection of George and Martha Washington memorabilia in America is displayed at the Smith-Harrison Museum (Depot Street, 205-669-4545). Who would ever expect to find items used at Mount Vernon in such a small town in Alabama? Yet the Mildred B. Harrison Library Building contains portraits, letters, china, and silver used at Mount Vernon and passed down over the years to sixth-generation direct descendant Charlotte Smith Weaver of nearby Chelsea. Two-thirds of the collection was donated back to Mount Vernon, but Columbiana banker Karl Harrison acquired the remainder of the collection in 1983 and opened the museum. Letters display the signatures of historical figures such as James Madison, Lord Cornwallis, and John Adams.

From Columbiana take State 25 west to **Calera,** home of the Heart of Dixie Railroad Museum (Ninth Street, 205-668-3435). Housed in the old depot, the museum has memorabilia such as schedule chalkboards from a Birmingham station that still have the times marked in. In the railroad yard are a working diesel engine and a steam tea-thermos engine for freight-yard switching. The latter engine didn't have a boiler, but worked from hot water poured into it. When the water was no longer hot, the engine stopped, so it was useful only in the rail yard. The most unusual piece of equipment is a Strategic Air Command (SAC) missile-control and guard car that always accompanied any SAC bomb or missile shipments.

The museum maintains five miles of track and offers rides in old passenger cars. Eventually there will be twenty-five miles of track. The Heart of Dixie Festival is a semiannual event held in October and April.

Continue west on State 25 to **Montevallo,** which is not only the geographic center of Alabama, but is also the home of the University of Montevallo. Although most folks go to college to get an education, you may want to stop by the university to look at the trees. The campus has so many different types of trees that a Tree Walk has been developed. Pick up a "Guide to Campus Trees" from the Chamber of Commerce (966 Main Street, 205-665-1519) and wander around the paths and off the marked trails. Of particular interest are the trees that are not normally found in this area. For

The gristmill at Tannehill Historical State Park

example, the Dahoon holly is usually found only along the streams and swamps near Mobile; the ginkgo is the only survivor of a group of trees that disappeared long ago from most of the earth; and the bald cypress occurs naturally in swamps and river banks along the coast. The Tree Walk is particularly spectacular in the spring and fall.

Drive by Flowerhill (35115 Flowerhill Drive), the residence of the university president. Built in 1926 on a hill surrounded by walkways and bountiful flowers, the building has a restored interior featuring numerous floral patterns and colors. The house is a gathering place for various college and community social occasions. The King House (Bloch and King Streets), which is used to house guests of the university, is an 1823 plantation house in which ghosts of the original owners are said to roam.

Montevallo's Aldrich Museum, located west of town on Shelby County 10 (205-665-2886), describes the history of coal mining. Cedar carvings enhance Orr Park, which is located one block east of downtown. Some years ago, several cedar trees in the park were extensively damaged in a storm and eventually died. Rather than cut down the dead trunks, Tom Tingle—a coal miner—carved them into figures of an owl, a squirrel, an Indian, and several faces. If you are exploring the quaint shops, take time for an elegant lunch or dinner at the Plaza Cafe (629 Main Street, 205-665-5461), which is well-known for steaks, seafood, white linen, and beautiful decor.

Go south on State 25 to Brierfield Iron Works Park (State 25, 205-665-1856), a component of Tannehill Historical State Park. Crumbling red brick walls are all that remain of the furnaces built in 1862 by the Bibb County Iron Company. In 1863 the Confederate government bought the iron works and added a second furnace and a rolling mill. It was reputed that the iron works produced the toughest and most suitable iron for making guns in the South. The furnaces towered sixty feet high and billowed black smoke into the sky. To feed these hungry furnaces, every tree for miles around was chopped down for charcoal. On March 31, 1865, less than two weeks before the end of the Civil War, Union troops rampaging through the countryside torched the furnaces.

In the 1880s, the furnaces were repaired, and during a brief boom period they produced tons of iron. Unfortunately, the metal furnaces in Birmingham could produce ten times as much per day, so in 1894 the furnaces cooled forever. Today the park is the site of a Civil War re-enactment in March as well as for weddings in the Mulberry

Church. The Brierfield Music Festival, also held at the park, is the first full weekend in May.

Head north on State 119 to I-65, where you will turn north to **Birmingham.** Named after the great industrial steel center in England, Birmingham is known as the Pittsburgh of the South. However, all that remains of the city's steel industry is the statue of Vulcan, the Roman god of the forge, and the Sloss Furnaces.

The only industrial plant of its size in the world that is being preserved, the Sloss Furnaces (First Avenue North Viaduct, 205-324-1911) furnished pig iron for Birmingham's foundries and mills for almost ninety years. Today it serves as a community center that showcases concerts and other performances as well as numerous fairs and festivals throughout the year.

Since 1938, *Vulcan*—the largest cast-iron statue ever made—has stood watch over the city from its own park (Twentieth Street South and Valley Avenue, 205-328-6198). A glass-walled elevator to the all-weather observatory affords a panorama of the formal gardens and a wide vista of the city.

Birmingham is only one of several cultural centers in Alabama, but it is probably the biggest. Recently re-opened after a major two-year renovation and expansion, the impressive Birmingham Museum of Art (2000 Eighth Avenue North, 205-254-2565) is the largest municipal museum in the Southeast, containing fifteen thousand works. The museum serves as a gateway to the Birmingham Cultural District, which includes the Civil Rights Institute, the Alabama Jazz Hall of Fame, and the Alabama Sports Hall of Fame (see The Road to Civil Rights chapter), as well as the Birmingham-Jefferson Civic Center, the opulent Alabama Theater, and Discovery 2000 (216 Nineteenth Street, 205-558-2000), which includes the Red Mountain Museum.

Five Points South, a historic neighborhood around Twentieth Street South, contains a rich collection of architecture as well as trendy restaurants, bars, shops, and a theater.

Other Birmingham attractions you might want to see include

Arlington Antebellum Home and Gardens (331 Cotton Avenue, 205-780-5656), the Birmingham Botanical Gardens (2612 Lane Park Road, 205-879-1227), the Birmingham Zoo (2630 Cahaba Road, 205-879-0408), the Southern Museum of Flight (4343 Seventy-third Street North, 205-833-8226), and the Alabama Museum of the Health Sciences (University of Alabama, 205-934-4475). Outdoors people enjoy the facilities at Oak Mountain State Park (off I-65, 205-663-6783) and Ruffner Mountain Nature Center (1214 South Eighty-first Street, 205-833-8264).

Birmingham residents are ardent sports fans. In addition to their passion for college sports, they support the Birmingham Barons Baseball Club, which plays at Hoover Metropolitan Stadium (100 Ben Chapman Drive, 205-988-3200). Horse and greyhound racing enthrall enthusiasts at the Birmingham Race Course (1000 John Rogers Drive, 838-7500), where visitors are eager to get to the starting gate for the only pari-mutuel horse racing in several states. A wide variety of wagering options are offered at the one-mile track where the racing continues rain or shine, day or night. Emphasis is on entertainment at the three-hundred-and-thirty-acre wooded site that includes seating for twenty-five hundred people, concession stands, restaurants, and lounges.

Birmingham bills itself as the city "that feels like a celebration," and its Festival of the Arts is the world's oldest and largest continuing arts celebration.

Called The Magic City, Birmingham boasts three grand historic hotels: the Tutwiler (Park Place at Twenty-first Street North, 205-322-2100 or 800-845-1787), the Holiday Inn–Redmont City Centre (2101 Fifth Avenue North, 205-324-2101 or 800-HOLIDAY), and the Pickwick Hotel (1023 Twentieth Street South, 205-933-9555 or 800-255-7304). However, all major hotel chains are also represented, and bed-and-breakfast accommodations can be arranged through Bed and Breakfast Birmingham (205-699-9841).

From Birmingham take I-59 southwest to **Bessemer,** named for Sir Henry Bessemer, the English pioneer who perfected the steel-

making process. Housed in the old 1916 Southern Railway Termi-
nal, the Bessemer Hall of History Museum (1905 Alabama Avenue,
205-426-1633) has displays that run the gamut from million-year-
old fossils to artifacts found in Indian mound excavations to Civil
War relics from the 28th Alabama Regiment. The Pioneer Room
contains articles from the 1800s including early school desks, fire-
fighting equipment, farm tools, a slave-made lazy-Susan table, and
early telephones.

All original structures, the Bessemer Pioneer Homes on Eastern
Valley Road are furnished with period pieces. At the 1840 McAdory
house and general store, the 1833 Owen house, and the 1818 Sadler
house, guides relate the stories of the Bessemer families and their
contributions to Alabama's early growth.

By the mid-twentieth century, Bessemer had become the home of
Pullman-Standard railroad cars and U.S. Pipe, one of the largest pipe
manufacturing plants in the world, but the city has never forgotten
the earlier debt it owes to steel.

Important annual events include the Greater Bessemer Festival of
Sacred Music in March, the Southern Appalachian Dulcimer Festi-
val in May, a Civil War re-enactment in September, and several
Christmas activities.

Go south on I-59 to Exit 100, where you head east toward
Bucksville. Watch for the signs to Tannehill Historical State Park
(12632 Confederate Parkway, 205-477-5711), a state memorial to
the history of iron and steel manufacturing in Alabama. Central to
the park located along scenic Roupes Creek are the remains of the
pre–Civil War Tannehill Ironworks. The cold-blast furnaces that
began Birmingham's iron industry could produce as many as twenty
tons of pig iron per day to provide iron for cannons, ordnance, skil-
lets, pots, and ovens for the Confederacy. The first furnace was built
in 1855, and the other two were added in 1863. On March 31, 1865,
just nine days before Lee surrendered to Grant at Appomattox, three
companies of Union cavalry plowed through the furnaces, blew up
the overhead trestles, tore up tramways, and burned the foundries,

cast houses, industrial buildings, tannery, sawmills, gristmill, brick works, and slave quarters. The molten metal hardened in the furnaces, where it remains to this day.

The entire site has been listed in the National Register of Historic Places and has been declared a National Metallurgical Engineering Landmark. Now called the Iron and Steel Museum of Alabama, the site features exhibits interpreting the history of technology up to 1865. The museum, which is a repository for early iron products and production machinery, is the South's largest assembly of such artifacts as rare ingot molds and cast boxes. Also located here is the Walter B. Jones Center for Industrial Archaeology.

Forty-five buildings that reflect life in Alabama during the mid-1800s have been reconstructed or moved to the site to create a pioneer village. The John Wesley Hall Grist Mill operated on the site from 1867 to 1931 on the banks of Mill Creek. A second-generation gristmill and cotton-gin operation, the original mill began operation on Mud Creek upstream from the furnaces before the Civil War but was burned by Union raiders. The old mill was reconstructed and turns out corn meal daily.

Other structures include an old country church, two schools, a country store, and the May Plantation Cotton Gin. Several pioneer cabins provide work and sales space for artisans such as the weaver, woodcarver, quilter, artist, potter, chairmaker, blacksmith, printer, and papermaker who are at the park on weekends from March through November.

Tannehill Farm is a collection of nineteenth-century farm buildings that includes the 1850 Williams house, a working blacksmith shop and sorghum mill, and the oldest building in the park, an 1822 dairy barn.

For the hardy the fifteen-hundred-acre park is laced with seven historic hiking trails such as the 1815 Bucksville-to-Montevallo Stagecoach Road, or visitors can use the Little Southern Railroad to get around the park.

Tannehill hosts several special events throughout the year, and on the third weekend of each month from March through November folks come to swap and sell at Tannehill Trade Days.

Accommodations are available in five historic rental cabins, a hundred and ninety-eight improved campsites, and fifty tent sites. Meals are available in Furnace Master's Inn, a cafeteria-style restaurant.

Created in 1972 by the Old Time Music Association to preserve and promote old-time country-and-western, bluegrass, and gospel music, the Tannehill Opry (Tannehill Parkway, 205-491-5955) features local and guest bands on Saturday nights.

Continue south on I-59 or the more leisurely US 11 to **Tuscaloosa.** Although the centerpiece of the city is the University of Alabama (the Crimson Tide), for the early history of Tuscaloosa you should go to the Old Tavern Museum (2800 University Boulevard, 205-758-8163). Built as a stagecoach stop in 1827, it is now the home of the Tuscaloosa Preservation Society and is also a museum with memorabilia from the days when Tuscaloosa was the capital of Alabama. The French influence is apparent in the wide overhanging roof line and the ironwork porch. The tavern has been relocated to Capitol Park, where you can wander around the ruins of Alabama's second capitol (1825-1846).

Although Tuscaloosa sustained tremendous damage during the Civil War, several houses survive and are open for tours. In Capitol Park is the McGuire-Strickland House (2828 Sixth Street, 205-758-2238). The 1820 wood-frame raised cottage is considered to be the oldest wooden structure in Tuscaloosa and is a well-preserved example of early Alabama workmanship as characterized by square nails, wooden pegs, and hand-hewn timbers that run the entire length of the house.

The Battle-Friedman House (1010 Greensboro Avenue, 205-758-6138) was the stately 1835 Greek Revival townhouse of Alfred Battle, a wealthy planter and businessman. Later, it was owned by Bernard Friedman, a Hungarian immigrant. Today, the beautifully restored and furnished mansion serves as a house museum and city cultural center.

Back on the university campus several of the beautiful buildings are open to the public. The Gorgas House (Capstone Drive, 205-

348-5906), built in 1829, is not only the oldest structure on campus, but also the oldest structure built by the State of Alabama and one of the first buildings in the state constructed specifically for the purpose of higher education. The raised Low Country cottage was originally a dormitory and dining hall, but later was occupied by the Gorgas family from 1879 to 1953. Even while the Gorgas family lived there, the house continued to be used as the university post office and as a hospital. General Gorgas served as the seventh president of the university, and his wife was the librarian for twenty-three years. Many family treasures are on display, including furniture and a large collection of colonial unalloyed silver called *plata de luna* because it is said to glow like the moon. The house is one of the most frequently copied homes in Alabama and appears in numerous books on Greek Revival and early American architecture.

Located in a 1909 neoclassical building, the Alabama Museum of Natural History (Smith Hall, University of Alabama campus, 205-348-2040) contains exhibits of natural history, geology, and mineralogy. Of special note are the fossils from the Coal Age, the age of dinosaurs, and the Ice Age.

In complete contrast, the Paul W. Bryant Museum (300 Paul W. Bryant Drive, 205-348-4668) is located in a contemporary building. Dedicated to the university's most-beloved coach, the late Paul "Bear" Bryant, the museum traces the history of Crimson Tide football since its inception in 1892. Highlights include memorabilia from Alabama's twelve national championship teams, Coach Bryant's famous houndstooth hat (and a replica of it in Waterford crystal), a re-creation of his office, and football art by Daniel Moore.

Drive by the president's home on University Boulevard. One of the four surviving buildings from the original campus, the outstanding Greek Revival house was spared during the Civil War burning of Tuscaloosa when the president's wife begged Union generals to spare it.

Several other important sights on the campus are the Denny Chimes, the Round House, the historic costume collection in Doster Hall, the replica of Hugo Black's study in the Law Library, and the Holtkamp Organ in the Frank Moody Music Building—one of the largest pipe organs in the Southeast.

You should also drive by the Dearing-Swain Home (2111 Fourteenth Street) which is considered to be the most perfect example of Greek-temple architecture in the state. Its walls are built of handmade clay bricks nineteen inches thick.

Tuscaloosa is the grateful beneficiary of one man's passion for fine art. Industrialist Jack Warner, CEO of the Gulf States Paper Corporation, has amassed an astounding personal collection of American art that includes sculpture, porcelains, paintings, and primitive artifacts. His collection is recognized as one of the most extensive collections of fine American art anywhere. However, rather than hoarding it, he shares the art with the public. Employees at the company headquarters (1400 River Road NE, 205-553-6200) are surrounded by a third of the works—a hundred and fifty pieces of art which range from primitive to modern—and the general public can tour the building in the evening and on weekends. The building is of oriental design and a tranquil Japanese garden occupies the courtyard.

Another third of the collection is displayed at the Mildred Warner House (1925 Eighth Street, 205-553-6200), named for Jack Warner's mother. Starting out in the 1820s as a simple one-story house, the building had a four-story brick portion added on in the 1830s. The exquisitely furnished home features antiques dating from 1700 to 1865. Paintings on exhibit include works by Edward Hopper, Mary Cassatt, and John Singer Sargent.

The final third of the collection is displayed at the North River Yacht Club, a private facility.

Probably the best children's museum we've seen anywhere is the Children's Hands-On Museum of Tuscaloosa (2213 University Boulevard, 205-349-4235). Enter a Choctaw Indian village through the Cave of Subtracting Years. In the village, children can make pottery and shell jewelry, play Choctaw games, and try out a dugout canoe.

T-Town gallery is a collection of businesses that were in Tuscaloosa at the turn of the century. Visitors can cash a check at the bank, buy trifles at the general store, print stationery or a bookmark at the print shop, or dress up in vintage clothing at Grandmother's Attic.

Move on to modern Tuscaloosa where there is a TV studio, a children's hospital, and a replica of a towboat wheelhouse. Climb through a rabbit hole or explore a large oak tree, make animal tracks at the mud table, or dig for treasures in the sand at Beavers' Bend, an indoor park. The museum also has a miniature planetarium and an extensive science department.

Tuscaloosa has many black heritage sites. Stillman College (3600 Fifteenth Street, 205-349-4240) was founded in 1876 to train black ministers. Among its Italian Renaissance structures is the 1881 college building.

An example of a pre-Depression-era home is the Murphy-Collins Home, residence of Tuscaloosa's first black morticians. Will Murphy went on to become a great black leader and businessman. The house contains black heritage memorabilia. Established prior to the Civil War, Prewitt Cemetery is the largest slave cemetery in the South.

While you're in the Tuscaloosa area, dine at the Cypress Inn (501 Rice Mine Road North, 205-345-6963), which is perched on a steep hillside overlooking the Black Warrior River. Have a drink or a snack on the outdoor patio surrounded by landscaped gardens.

Nearby historic downtown **Northport** is a mecca for artisans and antiques. At the Kentuck Art Center and Museum (501 Main Avenue, 205-333-1252), an artist's colony, you can visit the studios of potters, photographers, woodworkers, jewelry designers, glassblowers, a metalsmith, and a harpsichord maker. The museum features changing exhibits of contemporary and traditional American crafts and fine arts, with particular emphasis on the works of Alabama artists.

The annual Kentuck Arts Festival, held each October at Kentuck Park (3501 Fifth Street), is one of the South's premier arts fairs. Close to thirty thousand art lovers come to see the works of over two hundred artisans, as well as to enjoy storytelling, music, pioneer-skills demonstrations, and a variety of food items.

Take State 69 south to Moundville Archaeological Park (205-371-2572) on the Black Warrior River. The three-hundred-and seventeen-acre park is thought to have been the site of the largest and most powerful economic and ceremonial community of Native Americans during the Mississippian period (A.D. 1000-1500). Mississippian Indians built large earthwork mounds on which they constructed temples, council houses, and homes for the nobility. When a chief died, his buildings were burned and covered by another layer of earth, creating higher and higher mounds of which two dozen have survived.

Administered by the Alabama Museum of Natural History at the University of Alabama, exhibits at the park's museum chronicle the history of these ancient Native Americans through artifacts dug up during archaeological excavations of the site. At the museum you can watch a selection of short films about prehistoric Indians, and the daily lifestyle of the natives who lived here is also interpreted through a recreated temple on one of the mounds and an Indian village near the river. In addition, the park offers a boardwalk nature trail winding through the forest and along the river, as well as a thirty-one-space campground.

Whether your tastes run to fast cars, football, the Civil War, or even to the history of iron and steel production in the state, you'll find what you're looking for in central Alabama.

Calera Chamber of Commerce, P.O. Box 445, Calera, AL 35040, 205-991-4720.

City of Childersburg Chamber of Commerce, 118 Sixth Avenue SE, Childersburg, AL 35044, 205-378-5482.

Hardy Welcome Center, I-20, Heflin, AL 36264, 205-748-4303.

Montevallo Chamber of Commerce, P.O. Box 592, Montevallo, AL 35115, 205-665-1519.

Shelby County Economic Development Council, 1200 Corporate Drive, Hoover, AL 35238, 205-991-4720.

CHAPTER 8

LOOKOUT MOUNTAIN PARKWAY

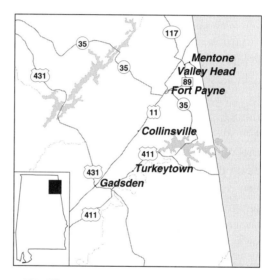

A veritable wonderland of scenic panoramas, waterfalls, caves, and fascinating rock formations, Lookout Mountain—the southern terminus of the Appalachian Mountains—extends eighty-three miles from Gadsden, Alabama, to Chattanooga, Tennessee, passing through a corner of northwest Georgia. Although the mountain's highest point is 2,393 feet at High Point, Georgia, the loftiest peak on the parkway in Alabama is 1,800 feet near Mentone, the second-highest spot in the state. The 100-mile highway running the length of the mountaintop is called the Lookout Mountain Parkway. This chapter is devoted to the Alabama portion of the parkway, which is 101 miles from north to south, including side excursions. A 67-mile hiking trail parallels the parkway.

Many of the roads in this area are county roads that don't always appear on large statewide maps. We suggest that you get the more detailed Lookout Mountain Parkway Travel Map either from the Lookout Mountain Parkway Association (address below), from a welcome center when you enter Alabama, or from any merchant once you get to one of the communities.

Lookout Mountain has one of the most abundant and varied plant communities in the world, with everything from soaring white oaks and chestnut oaks to rare orchids and pitcher plants concealed in secluded grottos. The whole length of the mountain itself is a riotous showcase throughout the seasons. Spring bursts forth with redbud and dogwood. Summer blossoms with mountain laurel, rhododendron, coreopsis, black-eyed Susans, and lobelia marching along the mountain roads. Autumn blazes with goldenrod and brilliant leaves. Many uncommon fern and mushroom species make the mountain their home. Climatically distinct from the rest of the state, the area boasts mild summer temperatures and is cold enough in winter for snow skiing.

The attractions of the outdoors draw most visitors to the lofty heights. There are thirteen summer camps along the parkway—a concentration greater than in any other area of the country—as well as magnificent caves, numerous state parks, hiking trails, family-owned fisheries, horse ranches, golf courses, a dude ranch, and a ski resort— you heard right, a ski resort. You can make a day trip or a week-long vacation out of a visit to Lookout Mountain. No wonder natives call the area the most "Wander-full" part of Alabama. So enticing is the mountain that all the members of the musical group ALABAMA live there—two near Mentone and two near Fort Payne.

Just shy of the Georgia state line at the intersection of State 117 and County 89, quaint **Mentone** is located high above it all atop the mountain. Mentone literally means "musical mountain spring." Just as you'd expect, the area abounds with natural cascades and gurgling brooks.

Mentone has everything you'd expect to find in a small hamlet perched above the clouds: crisp pollution-free air, clear streams, unimpeded vistas, cool temperatures, and blessed peacefulness. No flashing signs mar the landscape, nor are there shopping malls, fast-food joints, or traffic jams. If Mentone could be said to have an industry, it is summer camp. More than a dozen of them are hidden away in wooded glens.

Shops and restaurants are nestled together on one main street, which is State 117. Residential areas are reached by narrow, twisting lanes. Cottages are tucked here and there, almost invisible behind lush greenery. Many are located along the mountain's ridge (which locals call The Brow), where they overlook spectacular panoramas of the valley below. The best view of all is from the Mentone Brow Overlook just a short way down the road behind the century-old Mentone Springs Hotel (State 117, 205-634-4040), the focus of downtown. Built before the turn of the century as a mountain retreat, the hostelry was purchased during the 1920s by the Alabama Baptist Convention for its summer encampments. The next fifty years were checkered, but the hotel has been undergoing restoration since 1980.

Today, the majestic building houses Ye Olde Heritage House Restaurant and offers some bed-and-breakfast rooms. Rocking on the endless front porch affords you a view that goes on forever. The hotel's old annex, now called the White Elephant Galleries, contains several craft shops and galleries.

Crafts are a big business in Mentone. Many talented artisans and craftspeople have migrated to Mentone and made it their permanent home, drawing many seekers of original and handmade items there, too, in the process. The historic Hitching Post (State 117) and the Log Cabin Craft Village across the street feature many craft shops.

You'll want to sample the home cooking offered at several excellent restaurants in town. Dessie's Kountry Chef (State 117, 205-634-4232) is open for breakfast, lunch, and dinner and specializes in barbecue, Kountry-fried steak, and catfish. Vegetables are plentiful. Be sure to save room for the homemade buttermilk-coconut pie.

The century-old Mentone Springs Hotel

The Log Cabin Restaurant and Deli in the Craft Village (State 117, 205-634-4560) bills itself as Mentone's "Not-so-fast, yet always good restaurant." Located in an 1800 log cabin that once operated as an Indian fur trading post, the restaurant is open for lunch and dinner and offers something for every palate—sandwiches served on freshly baked breads, country ham, country-fried steak, and even Mexican dishes. Drinks are served in frosty Mason jars.

Cragsmere Manna (De Soto Parkway, 205-634-4677), located in what is reputed to be the oldest house on The Brow, is the closest you'll get to formality. The restaurant serves dinner on Friday and Saturday as well as Sunday brunch. In 1898 a former slave and his wife built a cabin on the site and began serving Sunday picnics for blacks and whites. The rustic, rambling building gradually evolved into its present form.

Mentone's colorful folklore is liberally sprinkled with real-life characters of old like Granny Dollar and Colonel Milford Howard, but today's residents are just as absorbing.

Granny Dollar was an intrepid Indian woman who lived to be approximately 105. Because she could neither read nor write, she wasn't sure of her birth date. Her family escaped being deported to Oklahoma via the infamous Trail of Tears in the 1830s by hiding in a cave. Both her father and her fiancé served in the Confederate army during the Civil War and were killed in the Battle of Atlanta.

By then a strapping six feet tall, she earned a living hauling wholesale goods to rural merchants. She didn't marry until she was seventy-nine and never had any children, but nonetheless earned the nickname Granny. The Dollars were married for twenty years, and when Nelson died, Granny sold her last cow to buy her late husband a tombstone. She spent her last years living in a cabin on the grounds of Col. Milford Howard's Master School. Although Granny had saved twenty-three dollars for her own tombstone, thieves stole the money during her funeral. A civic group erected a headstone for Granny in 1973, and money is currently being raised to reconstruct her cabin.

Colonel Howard came to Fort Payne in 1880 to begin practicing law. He married Sallie Lankford and was elected to Congress, then went to Hollywood, where he had a successful career as a scriptwriter.

When Sallie died she was buried in California, but Howard dreamed of a memorial for her on Lookout Mountain. The Sallie Howard Memorial Chapel (177 Parker Avenue SE, Rainsville, 638-4441) is built around a gigantic boulder that forms one end wall. After his death Howard's remains were cremated and placed inside the giant rock. The chapel is open at all times, and visitors are invited to "come as you are" to regular Sunday services.

A contemporary Lookout Mountain character is Jack Jones, the owner of Cloudmont Golf and Ski Resort and Shady Grove Dude Ranch. Jones, a long-time veteran of summer camp operation, first came to the mountain in 1926 as an eight-year-old camper and vowed to own a camp someday. He returned as an adult and bought a camp. He now owns almost everything in the vicinity of Mentone. At seventy-six years old, he runs a dude ranch (where he does the square-dance calling), a ski resort and a golf resort, and is an accomplished painter. He knows everybody and is full of tall tales of which he says, "I've told these stories so long I believe them myself."

Alabama's only dude ranch, Shady Grove Dude Ranch (County 165, 205-634-4344), is located on three thousand acres. Thirty horses tended by three cowboys carry visitors along the 100 miles of trails.

Simple accommodations are in several ranch buildings. Activities include horseback and wagon rides, cookouts, square dancing, and campfires in the hayloft.

The Saddle Rock Golf Course, also owned by Jack Jones, is open seven days a week from May through November. Play is on nine holes using eighteen tees. The first tee is from a spot on a huge boulder located 30 feet above the fairway. In 1970, Jones introduced snow skiing to Alabama and combined the two sports facilities into the Cloudmont Ski and Golf Resort (205-634-4344). Nine state-of-the-art snow machines pump out powder as soon as the temperature falls below twenty-eight degrees at night.

The Enchanted Gardens and Gallery (State 117, 205-634-4777), located just east of Mentone, is an unusual plant nursery. Indulge yourself in a leisurely stroll through the display gardens featuring a water garden surrounded by Japanese maples, conifers, and perennials. Regional fine arts and crafts are displayed inside the gallery, the exterior of which is adorned with a fantasy mural. The specialty-plant nursery sells hundreds of varieties of unusual plants and accessories.

Mentone brims with quaint places to lay down your head. Bonnie and Jim Schmidt welcome visitors to their Blossom Hill Bed and Breakfast and Herb Farm (205-634-4673 or 800-889-4244) located on Little River Canyon below DeSoto Falls. Accommodations are in a rustic four-unit guest cottage with all the modern amenities.

The Mentone Inn (State 117, 205-634-4836), situated right in the center of town, is a rustic, rambling 1927 inn with awning-shaded porches, a sundeck, separate cottages, a hot tub, table tennis, and horseshoes. Because it's unheated, it is open only from May to October. From MADAPERCA (State 117, 205-634-4792), you can awake to the sound of Little River passing over a historical dam. This bed and breakfast was fancifully named for four brothers and sisters—MAry, DAisy, PERcy, and CArl.

Special events will keep you coming back to Mentone. Spring brings the Rhododendron Festival. Scenic Brow Park is the site of the Mentone Crafts Festival in July. Fall Colorfest is the third weekend in October. What better place for an old-fashioned Christmas than Mentone?

Sequoyah Caverns (205-635-6423), also known as the Looking Glass Caverns, is located on US 11 near Valley Head. Named after the famous Cherokee Sequoyah, who invented the Cherokee alphabet, the caves contain hundreds of unusual formations and thousands of ancient fossils. The dramatically lit Looking Glass Lakes reflect these formations in crystal clear water. Towering stalagmites give the caverns the appearance of an underground palace.

Stay at Woodhaven Bed-n-Breakfast in **Valley Head** (205-635-6438). This historic 1902 farmhouse offers large bedrooms, each with a sitting area and a fireplace. Children are welcome and encouraged to get to know the farm animals.

Located on County 89 between Mentone and Fort Payne, De Soto State Park (Blaylock Drive, 205-845-5380 or 800-568-8840)—known as the Home of Mother Nature—features five thousand acres of pristine forest land, an abundance of wildlife and wildflowers, geologic landmarks, and scenic beauty stretching from De Soto Falls to Little River Canyon. Beginning near Mentone, the park meanders along 40 miles of roads and rivers to a point near Weiss Lake. First described by Hernando De Soto, the falls that bear his name plummet 100 feet from a mile-long, mirror-smooth lake into a rugged ravine. Indian fortifications once protected rock rooms in a nearby cliff.

Continue south on County 89 down off the mountain to **Fort Payne.** Recognized in Norman Crampton's *The 100 Best Small Towns in America*, Fort Payne is the sock capital of the world. Fort Payne alone produces more socks than any *country* in the world. The city is also home to Earth Grains, the largest non-bread bakery in the world, which specializes in hamburger buns and snack cakes.

Stretching along a scenic valley between Sand and Lookout Mountains in the Alabama Mountain Lakes Region, Fort Payne began as a stockade in which Native Americans were incarcerated before being sent to Oklahoma on the Trail of Tears. A chimney that was once part of the old fort is all that remains.

The ALABAMA Fan Club and Museum (201 Glenn Avenue South, 205-845-1646) celebrates the hometown country group ALABAMA. Watch a short film about the group members, then tour the exhibits of their gold records, awards, and personal memorabilia. During the benefit June Jam week sponsored by the group (it's the largest outdoor country-music festival in the world), ALABAMA performs along with other country-music notables, and you can tour the group members' homes. It's not unusual to see one or more of the band members at the museum, because they all live nearby and are active in running the venture.

Admission is free to the Depot Museum (Fifth Street NE, 205-845-5714) housed in the 1891 Richardson Romanesque Fort Payne depot, which was used as a passenger depot until the 1970s. The heavy pink sandstone facade sports turrets and arched windows. In front of the museum is a twenty-five-foot totem pole carved by Georgia chain-saw sculptor Jim Marbutt. His theme of "Live in Balance" is depicted through figures such as an eagle for freedom; a face representing the mystery of the spirit; three Indian heads depicting the Woodlands, Plains, and Southwest Indians; and a snake symbolizing the importance of staying in touch with the earth. A small exhibit of railroad memorabilia is housed in a red caboose located in front of the museum.

Inside, the exhibits include Indian artifacts, late-nineteenth-century farm equipment, photographs, artwork, historical items, hand-blown glass whimsies, and ninety dioramas depicting fairy tales and historical events.

The oldest theater in Alabama still in use, the Fort Payne Opera House (510 North Gault Avenue, 205-845-3957) was described as the most convenient and handsome opera house in the state when it was built in 1889. Over the last hundred years, the impressive structure has served as a movie house, a school auditorium, and a rehearsal hall and was also put to use as a place for square dances, baby contests, amateur nights, and professional stage shows. Although the opera house was closed from 1935 to 1969, the elaborate murals representing local history that adorn the walls leading to the towering stage have been rejuvenated. Today, the Landmarks of DeKalb Players and a monthly presentation called "Radiovisions" occupy the stage of the theater.

In addition to June Jam, other special events in Fort Payne include the DeKalb County Arts and Crafts Show held the second weekend in November, the DeKalb County VFW Agricultural Fair held the first week in October, and Fort Payne's mid-December Christmas in the Park and Christmas Parade.

Follow State 35 back up the mountain and take Canyon Rim Parkway twenty miles along the west rim of Little River Canyon. Recently designated a National Preserve, the canyon claims to be the deepest gorge east of the Rockies. Over eons the craggy 17-mile canyon was gashed through the rocky strata by the Little River, the only river in the country that runs its entire course on a mountain top. On the rim drive you'll enjoy overlooks, waterfalls, and breathtaking views. The best glimpse of Little River Falls is from where State 35 and Little River Canyon Rim Road cross the river.

Many actual events are just as fascinating as all the legends that abound about the canyon. Rangers have braved the canyon's sheer walls to rescue both humans and vehicles that have ended up in the canyon. You can watch a video of some of these exploits at the De Soto Park Lodge. White-water rafting and rappelling are permitted in the canyon, but permits are required.

A little farther south along State 35 is Weiss Lake, the Crappie Capital of Alabama. The lake's celebrity is revealed by the fact that more out-of-state fishing licenses are issued here than at any other site in Alabama. The 30,200-acre impoundment of the Coosa, Chatooga, and Little Rivers has more than 447 miles of shoreline. You can also reach the lake from Collinsville by State 68.

Retrace State 35 north to State 273. Follow State 23 south to State 68, then take State 68 to the Cherokee Rock Village Park, located off County 89 south of Collinsville. This imaginary village was created by Mother Nature from huge boulders of all sizes. From the maze of cracks, crevices, and caves formed by the enormous stones—some nearly 200 feet high—you'll get one of the best East Brow overlooks on Lookout Mountain. Part of the view includes Weiss Lake.

Continue north on State 68 to **Collinsville.** What began in the 1950s as barely more than a sale of coon dogs, bird dogs, and rabbit dogs has grown to become a legendary sale day of diverse items. Folks come from far and near to Collinsville Trade Day (205-524-2536). Trade Day is a cultural experience for the uninitiated. Held on Saturdays, it features one thousand vendors and attracts thirty thousand bargain hunters, swappers, and traders. Vendors sell from the beds of their pickup trucks, from booths, or from a patch of ground, yard-sale style. You'll find everything from goats to bent-can groceries to twig furniture to wholesale Bibles to hubcaps and cowboy boots. Still true to its roots, the sale continues to feature two-hundred pet vendors.

Head south on US 11 to **Gadsden,** which has long been an important crossroads. Both the routes Hernando De Soto took in 1540 and the trail used by General Andrew Jackson en route to battling the Creek Indians cross in Gadsden. The dividing line between the Cherokee and the Creek nations was nearby. The route taken by John Wisdom to warn the citizens of Rome, Georgia, that they were about to be attacked by Federal troops passed through Gadsden, and Wisdom's grave is just outside of town.

The best view in the area is from Paseur Overlook on Brow Drive, two blocks from Noccalula Falls Park (1500 Noccalula Road, 205-549-4663), which is Gadsden's most notable attraction and Alabama's largest and most-visited outdoor tourist site. The falls itself plunges off a rocky ledge and lands in a spray of mist 90 feet below. At the top of the falls, poised as if to leap over, stands a larger-than-life-size statue representing the Cherokee Indian maiden Noccalula. Legend says that she jumped to her death rather than marry a Creek warrior her father had chosen. Supposedly her heartbroken father then named the falls after her.

The history-rich Noccalula Gorge has been a tourist spot since the early 1800s, when Chalybeate Springs was visited for its healing and health-giving properties. So popular was the area in those days that a dancing pavilion was constructed under the falls and a streetcar line was built to bring in excursionists.

The park features an authentic two-hundred-year-old pioneer homestead with twenty-five buildings, a pioneer museum, the Gilleland-Reese Covered Bridge, botanical gardens containing twenty-five thousand azaleas, a miniature railroad, a small zoo stocked with native animals and fowl, a campground, and hiking trails.

In the ravine, the Historic Gorge Trail footpath skirts cascading streams and climbs alpine slopes and stretches of primitive back country. The trail allows you to explore caves and Indian carvings, an aboriginal fort, an abandoned dam, Chalybeate Springs, an old pump-house site from the Dwight Cotton Mill, Civil War carvings, rare plants, wildlife, and unusual rock formations with names such as Poor Man's Squeeze, Needle Eye, Mushroom Rock, Pyramid Rock, and Mystery Fort.

The park's parking lot serves as the end point of the World's Longest Outdoor Sale, which is held for four days each August along the 450-mile route from Covington, Kentucky, to Gadsden (800-

327-3945). Bargain hunters come from all over the United States and from as far away as Japan for this incredible shopping spree. Another special event is the Annual Noccalula Falls Park Antique Car Meet, held the third weekend in July. In addition to a display of over two hundred and fifty vintage automobiles, the event features a flea market, fashion show, and awards presentation.

Near the park is the Etowah County War Memorial. Dedicated in 1988, it is a tribute to Gadsden men who died in battle from World War I to the Lebanon War.

Gadsden sits in the Coosa River basin, former home of the Creek Indians, who were defeated in a battle with Andrew Jackson in 1814. You can take an exciting two-hour afternoon or dinner cruise aboard the *Alabama Princess* riverboat, an authentic eighty-foot-long replica of the picturesque excursion stern-wheelers that plied America's rivers during the last century. The boat is tied up at Riverside Boardwalk on US 411 South (300 Albert Rains Boulevard, 205-549-1111).

The Center for Cultural Arts (Fifth and Broad Streets, 205-543-2787) houses an art gallery, children's museum, dinner theater, concert hall, and a restaurant called Works of Art. The gallery regularly features traveling exhibits along with the works of local and regional artists. One of the highlights of the center is the world's largest site- and date-specific model railroad. Depicting Gadsden life in the 1940s and 1950s, the project is under constant renovation by the Coosa Valley Model Railroad Club. Six HO-scale trains travel through the town and countryside. The center is also home to the Gadsden Symphony and the Etowah Youth Orchestra.

Another part of the complex is Imagination Place, an outstanding hands-on museum designed for family fun that is really a child-sized city complete with a post office, hospital, supermarket, radio station, and fire station. Art classes, summer day camps, overnight sleep-ins, weekly activities for toddlers, children's theater productions, and science workshops are held regularly.

Admission is free to see the permanent collection of paintings, sculptures, and prints, as well as any traveling exhibits at the Gadsden Museum of Arts (2829 West Meighan Boulevard, 205-546-

7365). The Fowler Memorial Collection features European Impressionism, contemporary art, and whimsical assemblages of sculpture, antique china, and crystal. The historical collection includes Native American artifacts, textiles, costumes, photographs, tools, and a complete turn-of-the-century doctor's office.

The Emma Sansom monument—in the center of Broad Street at the corner of First Street—honors a young girl who became a heroine during the Civil War by leading General Nathan Bedford Forrest and his men away from a Union ambush.

You can walk or drive through the Ohatchee Creek Wildlife Park on US 431 South (205-892-2361 or 205-442-1453) to see tigers, giraffes, kangaroos, zebras, and other exotic animals.

The Corn Crib Corner Country Crafts Shop (1405 Elliott Road, 205-546-2040) is one of those off-the-beaten-track shops that seem to be a million miles from civilization. The building itself is an old barn. Wood furniture, quilts, baby gifts, signs, and other items are made by family members and local craftspeople.

During May's Riverfest, the city comes alive with gospel singers, street dances, talent shows, children's events, and sporting competitions. In December, the river sparkles with colored lights as brilliantly bedecked boats parade by as part of Lights on the Coosa.

Nearby historical sites include Turkeytown, the capital of the Cherokee nation; Civil War battle sites at Black Creek, Turkeytown, and Kings Hill; and the world's first hydro-electric generator site.

The annual Cherokee Indian Powwow and Green Corn Festival is the third weekend in August at Turkeytown (US 411, 5.5 miles north of US 278). This celebration of Native American heritage features traditional, intertribal, and competitive dancing to the beat of native drums. Also featured are lifestyle demonstrations, storytelling, music and song, arts and crafts, sacred literature, and Indian traders offering a wide range of goods and services from tribal food to face painting.

The wonders of the Lookout Mountain Parkway beckon visitors throughout the year. Explore the parts of the parkway in Georgia and Tennessee as well to do the whole area justice.

Alabama Welcome Center, I-59, Collinsville, AL 35961, 205-635-6522.

DeKalb County Tourism Association, 2201 J. Gault Avenue North, Fort Payne, AL 35967, 205-845-3957.

Fort Payne Chamber, 300 Gault Avenue North, Fort Payne, AL 35967, 205-845-2741.

Gadsden-Etowah Tourism Board, 1500 Noccalula Road, Gadsden, AL 35901, 205-549-0351.

Lookout Mountain Parkway Association, P.O. Box 288, Mentone, AL 35984, 205-634-4344.

CHAPTER 9

ON THE
TRAIL OF LOST
LUGGAGE

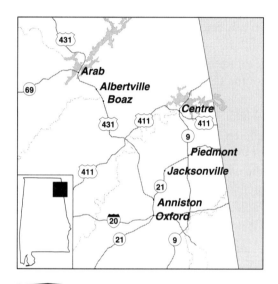

Covered bridges, an Indian maiden, shop-till-you-drop browsing, and lake activities vie with angels, prehistoric creatures, and lost luggage along the 152-mile US 431/State 1 route slashing through mountainous northeast Alabama.

Begin at **Oxford,** located just north of I-20. Tranquil Oxford Lake Park is the site of the historic Coldwater Covered Bridge. Nearby is the Olde Mill Antique Mall (100

117

Mill Street, 205-835-0599), the largest antique mall in the Southeast. More than 150 dealers in antiques and collectibles await you in the one-hundred-year-old cotton mill. Along Mill Street you'll find former mill cottages brimming with more goodies.

Head north on US 431/State 1 to **Anniston.** The Model City of the South was founded in 1872 by industrialist Samuel Noble, who named most of the streets after Episcopal bishops.

A tribute to Old World architecture, the 1888 romantic Romanesque Church of St. Michael and All Angels (West Eighteenth Street at Cobb Avenue, 205-237-4011) was donated to the working people of Anniston by John Ward Noble. The architect for the project was William Hulsey Wood, who drew the original plans for the Cathedral of St. John the Divine in New York City.

In-so-far as possible, local materials were used to create the church with its Norman and Gothic influences. True to its name, the church has angels everywhere. Angel heads at the ends of ceiling beams are positioned so that each one is appropriately placed to face the altar. A statue of St. Michael is flanked by statues of the archangels Gabriel and Raphael, who are surrounded in turn by niches surmounted by seven angels bearing symbols of events in Christ's life.

The church also features a 95-foot bell tower with twelve bells, the heaviest of which weighs 4,350 pounds; brilliant stained-glass windows, one of which is a Tiffany window; a twelve-foot-long white Carrara marble altar; a hand-carved ceiling that is an exact replica of a ship's ribs; and a magnificent 1889 organ with 2,715 pipes and seventy-three stops.

Anniston boasts several historic districts. Tyler Hill District is centered on a rising crest that peaks at a small park surrounded by a dozen extravagantly built Victorian homes. The other districts are the East Anniston Residential Historic District, Glenwood Terrace Historic District, West Fifteenth Street Historic District, and the Downtown Anniston Historic District.

Expect the unexpected around every corner at the Anniston

Museum of Natural History (800 Museum Drive, 205-237-6766). The largest city-funded natural history museum in the Southeast, it boasts one of the nation's most extensive collections of natural history specimens. The best feature of this museum is that most displays have been taken out from behind glass cases, which increases their impact on visitors.

Each hall offers a blend of realistic displays combined with graphics, sounds, educational labels, and hands-on experiences. The Dynamic Earth display, which chronicles the formation of our ever-changing planet, features a meteorite, dazzling gemstones, and a hurricane ball, as well as a re-created Pteranodon flying over a twenty-foot-long Albertosauros and fossilized plants and animals millions of years old. Dripping stalactites, cave-dwelling life forms, and dank, cool air introduce you to Underground Worlds.

The struggle for survival is the focal point of Attack and Defense, where you'll see how different animals find food or defend themselves. This exhibit includes North American mammals, live snakes, and a working honeybee colony.

Designs for Living is one of the nation's oldest diorama bird collections. Assembled around the turn of the century, the displays boast hand-painted habitat settings. Because of the age of the collection, you'll be able to see extinct species such as the passenger pigeon and Carolina parakeet as well as the endangered whooping crane and the red-cockaded woodpecker.

In Adaptations to the Environment, located in Lagarde African Hall, you can go on a safari and have a close encounter with more than a hundred African animals in a re-created natural savannah environment that includes a life-size model of an enormous baobab tree.

On the grounds of the museum are a wildlife garden, the Eugenia G. Brannon Nature Trail, and the Bird of Prey Trail.

In Anniston stay or eat at The Victoria (Quintard Avenue, 205-236-0503 or 800-260-8781), an elegant Queen Anne Victorian mansion built in 1888. Perched on a wooded hillside—the highest spot in town—the house features a three-story turret, brilliant

The JAX National Balloon finals in October

stained-glass windows, a conservatory, and colonnaded verandas. Inside features include high ceilings and original hardware, mantels, flooring, and woodwork. The first floor has four individual dining rooms, a piano lounge, and a glass-enclosed veranda. Upstairs are three opulent antique-filled guest rooms.

A new three-story addition to the mansion wraps around the courtyard and pool. Each of the units is furnished with antiques and reproductions. The historic guest house has been converted to a one-bedroom suite featuring a whirlpool bath, wet bar, and doors opening onto a private patio and pool.

The carriage house functions as the studio of noted wildlife painter Larry K. Martin and as the Wren's Nest Gallery (205-238-0710), which is the exclusive international distributor of his work. Martin—whose works have been exhibited at the National Wildlife Federation, the Audubon Naturalists Society, and the Governor's Mansion in Montgomery—designed the 1985 Alabama Waterfowl Stamp which features his rendition of a pair of wood ducks. Another popular series he's working on is "characters and eccentrics" portraits.

Just north of Anniston, still on US 431/State 1, is Fort McClellan, dubbed the "Military Showplace of the South." Completed in 1917, the forty-six-thousand-acre base—one of the nation's most beautiful—is home to three military museums.

The U.S. Army Chemical Corps Museum (Building 2299, 205-848-3355 or 205-848-4449) traces the history of the department that began in 1917 as the Chemical Warfare Service. However, exhibits also trace the use of chemicals all the way back to the Greeks and Romans. The museum features more than four thousand chemical warfare offensive and defensive artifacts. Some of the most interesting displays are the gas masks. Beginning with World War I, masks were developed not only for adults and children, but also for dogs and even horses.

The U.S. Army Military Police Corps Regimental Museum (Building 3182, 205-848-3522 or 205-848-3050) chronicles the history of the Military Police. The Military Police Corps was not established as a separate combat-service support branch of the army until 1941, but provost guards have existed since the Revolutionary War. The large collection includes firearms, period uniforms, Civil War photographs and artifacts, combat art from World War I to Vietnam, and military vehicles such as a V-100, personnel carrier, a helicopter, and a river patrol boat.

Uniforms, photographs, and exhibits at the Women's Army Corps Museum (Building 1077, 205-848-3512) trace women's roles in the U.S. Army from the Revolutionary War through the inception of the Women's Army Auxiliary Corps in 1942 to the present. Exhibits illustrate the barracks life of a WAC, duties in military units, and life overseas and at U.S. posts, as well as display awards, decorations, uniforms from fatigues to bloomers to stylish evening dress.

After leaving Fort McClellan, take State 21 north to **Jacksonville.** Dr. Francis's Museum and Apothecary (Gayle Avenue, 205-435-7611) is considered to be one of the finest examples of a mid-nineteenth-century professional office in the state. Displays from the days of "bite the bullet" feature authentic antebellum medical and pharmaceutical objects. Also in Jacksonville, the 1858 First Presbyterian Church served as a hospital during the Civil War.

Jacksonville and Anniston share the sponsorship and activities of the JAX National Balloon Finals each October. Balloon competitions, a parade of lights, a concert, and tethered balloon rides are among the activities.

Continue north on State 21 to **Piedmont,** the site of a devastating tornado in the spring of 1994. The Cross Plains Depot, known as the Crossroads of the Southeast during the 1880s, is now the Piedmont Museum (208 North Main Street, 205-447-6904), which exhibits memorabilia from 1838 to the present. Dedicated to the victims of the 1986 Challenger disaster, Piedmont Challenger Park (West Memorial Drive off State 21) is filled with granite monuments.

Go north on State 9 to **Centre.** Visit the Cherokee County Historical Museum (101 East Main Street, 205-927-8455 or 205-927-7835), which houses five thousand items dating from the mid-1800s, including washtubs and household appliances, farm tools, a blacksmith shop, weapons, newspapers, daguerreotype photographs from 1831 to the present, records, wagons, railroad memorabilia, and other artifacts pertaining to the history of the area.

The gigantic boulders of the Cherokee Rock Village are described in the Lookout Mountain Parkway chapter.

Nearby Weiss Lake (US 411/State 9, 205-927-8455) is known as The Crappie Capital of the World. Anglers consistently reel in two-pound fish, but the record catch was five pounds, two ounces. Shallow flats, underwater drop-offs, deep channels, large coves, stump flats, sloping points, weed beds, and strong feeder creeks combine to make the 447-mile lake an ideal home for crappie, bream, shad, and crawfish.

Even though the sights around Centre are entertaining, the real reason to visit the small town is Muffins Cafe (US 411 South, 205-927-2233). Billed as "lost in the '50s," the restaurant is filled with fifties' keepsakes, racing souvenirs, Hollywood mementos, and autographed pictures of all the famous people who have eaten there. The luncheon menu features enormous quantities of the vegetables of the day, while the dinner menu includes sandwiches, steaks, and seafood.

Leave Centre by taking US 411 to Gadsden, which is described in the Lookout Mountain Parkway chapter.

From Gadsden, take US 431 north to **Boaz,** which is located on scenic Sand Mountain. "Shop till you drop" is the rallying cry of this small town known far and wide for its shopping bargains. Boaz Shopper's Paradise (Billy B. Dyar Boulevard at State 68, 205-593-8154) contains a hundred and forty outlet stores offering direct-from-manufacturer prices.

If an airline has ever lost your luggage, you know how frustrating that experience can be. Some baggage is never reunited with its owner. So what happens to it? Some of it ends up at a place like the Unclaimed Baggage Center (101 East Bartlett, 205-593-4393), where the items are sold off at bargain prices.

Get back on US 431/State 1 and go north to **Albertville.** The Albertville Train Depot Museum (Sand Mountain Drive, 205-878-3821) honors the iron horse through displays like the two scale-model railroads that fill the depot's freight yard and the railroad memorabilia found in the Red Caboose Museum.

Continue north on US 431/State 1 to Guntersville, which is covered in the Tennessee River Heritage chapter.

Take State 69 west to **Arab.** The Arab Historic Complex (Arab City Park, 205-586-8413) is a collection of historic buildings that includes the 1935 Old Hunt School and a 1912 church.

From here you could continue on State 69 to Cullman and pick up the sights described in the Bridging the Gaps chapter, ending up in Phil Campbell; or you could even continue north of there to The Shoals, described in the Tennessee River Heritage chapter.

Alabama Mountain Lakes Association, 25062 North Street, Mooresville, AL 35649, 205-350-3500.

Albertville Chamber of Commerce, 316 Sand Mountain Drive, Albertville, AL 35950, 205-878-3821.

Arab Chamber of Commerce, 1157 North Main Street, Arab, AL 35016, 205-586-3138.

Boaz Chamber of Commerce, 306 West Mann Avenue, Boaz, AL 35957, 205-593-8154.

Cherokee County Chamber of Commerce, 590 East Main Street, Centre, AL 35960, 205-927-8455.

Marshall County Tourism, 200 Gunter Avenue, Guntersville AL 35976, 205-582-7015.

CHAPTER 10

THE SWINGING
SOUTH TRAIL

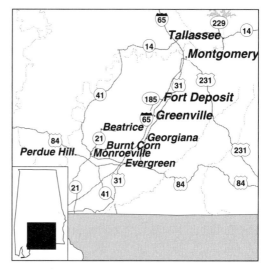

A lthough that world-renowned southern hospitality is abundant all over
Alabama, the warm, generous quality is honed to a fine point in the
southern part of the state. With the exception
of Montgomery, which we'll describe in this
chapter, and Mobile (described in The
Coastal Circle Tour), this region is characterized by small towns with big hearts and an
endless variety of attractions.

We'll begin this 261-mile southern odyssey east of Montgomery and amble south to the Monroeville area. If you want to start your excursion on a full stomach, begin at **Tallassee,** a small town just a few minutes north of I-85 at the junction of State 14 and State 229. The undisputed highlight of the town is the Talisi Hotel and Restaurant (14 Sistrunk Avenue, 334-283-2769). Nearly the entire ground floor space is consumed by the hotel's restaurant. Folks drive from as far as fifty miles away to chow down on the home-style cooking served at the sumptuous daily lunch buffet and Sunday buffet.

For more information about the area, visit the Chamber of Commerce (301 King Street, 334-283-5151), which is housed in a restored Confederate officers quarters.

From Tallassee take State 14 west to **Wetumpka.** Turn north on State 9 to Morrione Vineyards (3865 Central Plank Road, 334-567-9957). Tucked away at the very southern tip of the Blue Ridge Mountain chain are the small-operation's muscadine vines—native only to the Southeast—as well as the winery and tasting room.

Return south on State 9 to US 231 and head south. Watch for the signs for Jasmine Hill Gardens. Known as Alabama's Little Corner of Greece, Jasmine Hill Gardens and Outdoor Museum (1500 Jasmine Hill Road, 334-567-6463) boasts seventeen acres of gardens accented by thirty reproductions of Greek statues, fountains, and a full-scale reproduction of the Temple of Hera ruins. The 1830s cottage within the gardens was the owner's home.

At the Al Holmes Wildlife Museum (1732 Rifle Range Road, 334-567-7966) six hundred different species of animals—including lions, tigers, sharks, and other exotic creatures—are displayed in natural habitats. You can see live animals such as white-tailed and sika deer, foxes, skunks, and others.

Fort Toulouse/Jackson Park, set on a hundred and sixty-five acres at the junction of the Coosa and Tallapoosa Rivers (off US 231 North, 334-567-3002), features archaeological excavations, a museum, and partial reconstructions of the two historic forts held at different times by the French and the British.

The drugstore soda fountain at Old Alabama Town

Continue south on US 231 to **Montgomery.** The capital of Alabama presents a legacy of American history from conquistadors to Confederates. The city became the capital of Alabama in 1846 and served briefly as the capital of the Confederacy.

Begin a tour of Montgomery with a stop at the Montgomery Visitors Center (401 Madison Avenue, 334-262-0013), a restored 1850s residence at the edge of Old Alabama Town (310 North Hull Street, 334-240-4500). This complex, located near the heart of downtown in the Old North Hull Street District, features relocated historic homes and commercial buildings and costumed guides who depict urban and rural life between 1800 and 1900.

Recently restored, the stunning Alabama State Capitol (Bainbridge Street at Dexter Avenue, 334-242-3750) reveals a hundred and forty years of changing trends in architecture and furniture.

Visit the First White House of the Confederacy (644 Washington Avenue, 334-242-1861), which houses many of Jefferson Davis's personal belongings and Civil War memorabilia.

In addition to the black heritage/civil rights exhibits at the Alabama Department of Archives and History (see the Black Heritage chapter), the nation's first Archives and History Museum displays Native American and pioneer relics as well as Hank Williams memorabilia.

The Scott and Zelda Fitzgerald Museum (919 Felder Avenue, Apartment B, 334-264-4222) is in the house where the famous couple lived in 1931 and 1932. This is the only museum in the country dedicated to either of the celebrated duo.

A cultural giant, Montgomery is home to the Alabama Shakespeare Festival (One Festival Drive, 334-271-5353 or 800-841-4ASF)—the centerpiece of William M. Blount Cultural Park—and the Montgomery Museum of Fine Arts (One Museum Drive, 334-244-5700).

Country-music legend Hank Williams launched his career in Montgomery, and the Hank Williams Memorial (1304 Upper Wetumpka Road in the Oakwood Cemetery Annex) marks the final resting place of the crooner. The Hank Williams Museum across the street (334-264-4938) contains memorabilia from Williams's career. The six-foot-two-inch Hank Williams Statue is located in Lister Hill Plaza behind the Madison Hotel facing City Hall.

The Montgomery Zoo (329 Vandiver Boulevard, 334-240-4900) features habitats from five continents with natural, barrier-free environments for over eight hundred animals.

It's hard to choose where to stay in Montgomery. Several suggestions are the historic Riverfront Inn (200 Coosa Street, 334-834-4300), located in a restored freight depot; Red Bluff Cottage (551 Clay Street, 334-264-0056), a historic bed and breakfast; or Colonel's Rest (11091 Atlanta Highway, 334-215-0380), a country bed and breakfast.

For the next four towns on our tour—Fort Deposit, Greenville, Georgiana, and Evergreen—you can either take I-65 south or, if you prefer a more sedate pace, take US 31.

Fort Deposit is the home of Priesters Pecans (800-277-3226). For sixty years the company has been famous for its homemade candies and baked goods, many laden with pecans. The Kernel's Store, located at Exit 142 where I-65 and State 185 intersect, is a rustic general store selling Priester's sweets. A window in the Candy Kitchen allows guests to watch hand dipping of chocolates and pulling of brittle candies. In addition to the yummy samples, gifts are available for purchase, and there is a small sandwich bar.

South of Fort Deposit is **Greenville,** The Camellia City. Established as an agricultural center in 1816 near where the Old Federal Road and Bartram Trail converge at the site of Fort Dale, Greenville has a rich heritage. Get a brochure from the Chamber of Commerce (110 Cedar Street, 334-382-3251 or 800-959-0701) for a walking or driving tour that explores the historic downtown and residential neighborhoods full of gorgeous turn-of-the-century homes.

Two bed-and-breakfasts offer delightful accommodations. Rabbit Run Bed and Breakfast (State 185, 334-382-9719), a stately twenty-five-year-old Georgian house in a beautiful pastoral setting just off I-65, offers two spacious guest suites decorated with antiques. Pine Flat Bed and Breakfast (State 10, 334-346-2739), located out in the country on US 10 between Greenville and Pine Apple, was built in 1825 by an ancestor of the present owner. Magnificently restored heart-pine floors, grand fireplaces, American primitive pieces, English and German country antiques, and fresh flowers exude warmth and southern hospitality. Ralph Stacy of the Greenville Chamber of

Commerce describes the breakfast served at Pine Flats as a "two-thirds breakfast table." He explains that he means two-thirds of the table is covered with the food to be served. Pine Flats also offers hiking trails, horseback riding, and hay rides.

Special events in Greenville include the Watermelon Jubilee the second weekend in August and Christmas on Watermelon Hill in late November.

Continue south to **Georgiana** to visit the Hank Williams Museum (127 Rose Street, 334-376-9507) inside the 1850 boarding house that was the home of country music legend Hank Williams Sr. and his mother from 1930-1934, when Hank was between five and ten years old.

The memorabilia on display—all of which was donated by fans—traces Williams's musical odyssey from playing the guitar on the front porch in the summer and under the house in the winter to his success on the Louisiana Hayride and at the Grand Ole Opry. Crooner of such country classics as "Your Cheatin' Heart," "I Saw the Light," "Lonesome Whistle Blues," and "Hey Good Looking," Williams did most of his work in just three years before he was killed in a car accident. The house is overflowing with an extensive collection of 78-, 45-, and 33 1/3-rpm records, books, posters, stand-up displays, a Victrola, pictures, paintings, product endorsements, and sheet music.

The Hank Williams Sr. Day Celebration, which features country-music concerts and other activities, is held the first Saturday in June in the park behind the house.

Continue south to **Evergreen,** where you can shop at Ye Old Railway Emporium (100 Depot Square, 334-578-1707), a consignment shop that features the work of local artisans. Wooden doll cradles, playhouse furniture, bird feeders, quilt tacks, quilts, wall hangings, and the shop's own cookbook are just a few of the items on display. If the shop isn't open, someone from the Chamber of Commerce will be happy to let you in.

Take County 20 west to County 15, where you will turn north to **Burnt Corn.** Tourist associations and even travel writers tend to overuse the phrase "the town that time forgot" when describing little-changed historic villages. However, Burnt Corn really deserves the title. The ground on which the town was built was the site of the first battle of the Creek Indian War of 1814, and Andrew Jackson brought his army through on his way to fight the Battle of New Orleans. The Watkins House was built in 1812. The general store and post office have been in continuous operation since 1908. Other surviving buildings include the Baptist and Methodist churches, several historic homes, and some abandoned commercial buildings.

From Burnt Corn take County 30 west to **Peterman,** which has a historic railroad depot and an old commercial street. There's not much going on in Peterman most of the time, but the tiny crossroads is well known for its fall street festival.

Go south on State 21 to **Monroeville,** the county seat of Monroe County. Organized in 1815 and named after President James Monroe, the county's original size was once nearly half of Alabama's total area.

The lovely old courthouse on the town square in Monroeville was built in 1903 and served the county for fifty-nine years. Today, it houses the Chamber of Commerce and the Monroe County Heritage Museum (Downtown Square, 334-575-7433). You may recognize the courtroom with its swiveling jury chairs and pressed-tin ceiling embellished with a dogwood in each square. The entire room was replicated for the movie set of *To Kill a Mockingbird,* which was based on the Pulitzer Prize-winning novel written by Monroeville native Nelle Harper Lee. Dramatic productions of the work are performed periodically in the courtroom. The museum sponsors major exhibits that change four times per year. These displays primarily illustrate Monroe County's colorful past. The gift shop features works by local artists and craftspeople.

Monroeville is justly proud of its literary ties. In addition to being the birthplace of Harper Lee, Monroeville can also boast that Truman Capote drew much of his inspiration from the town. As a child he often visited his aunts there during the summer or on long school holidays, and Monroeville is featured in his stories "A Christmas Memory" and "The Thanksgiving Visitor."

Before Monroeville residents realized that they were losing some of their most significant buildings, the houses of both authors were torn down. However, the tide of destruction was stemmed before it became critical. Drive through the lovely neighborhoods of immense antebellum and Victorian homes. South Mount Pleasant Street has a particularly attractive collection of Victorian mansions.

As of yet there are no bed and breakfasts in Monroeville. Recommended places to eat include the Sweet Tooth Bakery, which serves a buffet lunch; Radley's Deli; and David's Catfish, which is also famous for its coleslaw.

Take County 47 southwest out of town to Mexia, where you will go west on US 84/State 12 to **Perdue Hill,** a small country crossroads with several historic homes and churches.

Perdue Hill has actually replaced the community of Claiborne, which was located just west of the present town. Fort Claiborne was established in 1813 as a supply base during the Creek Indian war and as a refuge for settlers during Indian attacks. It was designated the county seat of Monroe County in 1815.

Early writers describe Claiborne as an enchanting town situated on a level plateau high above the Alabama River. According to early resident Justus Wyman, "Fort Claiborne, as an inland town, stands unrivaled, and little doubt can be entertained of its being eventually one of the first commercial and political places in the territory." At one time the chief cotton port on the Alabama River, Claiborne had a cotton slide that was two hundred steps tall. During its glory days the town was a candidate for the state capital and boasted thirteen newspapers, as well as hotels, stores, taverns, a gin factory, a leather tannery, a furniture factory, a silversmith shop, and an academy.

Two state governors came from Claiborne—John Murphy and Arthur P. Bagley—and another worked there, although he lived across the river. James Dellett—a judge, U.S. Congressman, and Alabama's first Speaker of the House—built an impressive home in Claiborne around 1838.

Apparently early settlers thought that locating the town 150 feet above the river, away from the pest-ridden lowlands and swamps, would protect them from malaria and yellow fever. However, the town was plagued by both diseases, and many citizens moved away. The development of the railroads at the turn of the century spelled the doom of Old Claiborne, which was not on any railroad line. Today, Claiborne is not considered a ghost town or even a deserted town; it is a lost town. The only evidence that it ever existed are Dellett's home and the overgrown Claiborne Cemetery, which is reached by taking the last right turn before you cross the river.

Two Old Claiborne buildings that survived were moved to Perdue Hill. The most significant structure is the Masonic Lodge. Built between 1823 and 1827, it is the oldest documented public building in Alabama. Erected with funds from a public lottery, it stood at the west end of Claiborne's main street overlooking the river and Claiborne Common and functioned as both the Masonic hall and the county courthouse. In 1825 the Marquis de Lafayette addressed the citizens of Claiborne and Monroe County from a pulpit still in the hall.

Following the decline of Old Claiborne, the Masons dismantled the building and rebuilt it in its present spot in 1884. Over the years the old structure has served as a town hall, school, and church; but today it operates as a museum with displays that include a wealth of wonderful old photos illustrating life in the area (with special emphasis on old river boats), as well as odds and ends relating to the area's early history.

Located on the grounds of the lodge is another historic building that was also moved from Old Claiborne. The two-room William Barrett Travis Cottage served as both house and office to the lawyer William Barrett Travis, who gained fame as a commander at the Alamo, where he died. Travis had moved to Texas in 1831 because of his involvement in a mysterious affair of the heart. The original chair rail, wainscoting, paneled doors, and other architectural details are quite refined for such an early building.

Another historic building in Perdue Hill is the W.S. Moore Store. Located on its original site, it was built in 1875 as a doctor's office and then enlarged around 1927 for a store. It is a wonderful example of nineteenth-century commercial architecture. To the rear of the building is a privy built in 1890.

A side trip out of Monroe County takes you northwest along US 84/State 12—known in these parts as the "Corridor Through History"—past Gosport, Suggsville, Whatley, and finally to Grove Hill. An antebellum planter community, **Gosport** survived the Civil War due to its proximity to the river. River commerce got Gosport through Reconstruction, but the town's demise came with the advent of the railroad in the late 1800s, which bypassed Gosport. **Suggsville,** the antebellum cultural center of Clark County, also deteriorated after the Civil War.

Between Gosport and Whatley you'll cross Old Line Road/County 35. Legend says that the Creek and Choctaw Indians used this watershed line as the dividing line of their hunting grounds. In contrast to Suggsville's decline, **Whatley** boomed because of the iron horse. You can still see the remains of the Whatley Hotel, which was once a temporary home to salesmen and railroad workers. Unfortunately, Whatley eventually declined with the decrease in rail transportation in this century.

In **Grove Hill** the 1854 Alston-Cobb House has been restored for use as the Clarke County Museum (at the intersection of US 84 and US 43, 334-275-8684). Admire the 1840s Italianate Dickinson-Webb House across the street. Behind the museum is the John Gates Creagh Law Office. Built in 1834, it is one of the oldest surviving private law offices in Alabama.

Return to Perdue Hill on US 84/State 12 and turn north on County 39 to Fountain then turn north on State 41 to **Franklin,** a sleepy village with a historic church and a grocery store/post office where you can sit around the old woodstove to hear tales about the area. Ask about the casket in the loft.

Turn onto County 49 at the Haines Island Park sign where one of Alabama's two free ferries crosses the Alabama River to **Packer's Bend,** a historic black community famous for the quilts its women produce. The park contains picnic tables and a scenic overlook.

Retrace your route on State 41 to Fountain, where you will go east on County 42 to **Tunnel Springs.** Nearby is the 1837 Scotland Church and cemetery, which are all that remains of a community settled by Georgians and Carolinians. The land reminded the settlers of their native country. On the fifth Sunday of a summer month, descendants of the original residents hold a reunion on the grounds.

Turn north on State 21 to State 265. Just past **Beatrice,** look for the signs to Rickard's Mill, which is nestled in the piney woods along the banks of Flat Creek. First built in 1845 by an industrious German immigrant named Jake Rickard, the water-powered grist mill was relocated just south of its original site in 1858 after the initial location was washed out by flooding. The mill, which has been restored and is 65 percent original, is of board-and-batten construction with native cypress shingles.

The mill is now the centerpiece of a living history museum located within an 8.5-acre recreational park. A Leffel water turbine turns the millstones, and you can purchase freshly ground flour, corn, and grits or bring your own grain to be ground. Inside the mill are many of the original tools Jake Rickard made.

Owned continuously by the same family until the county acquired it, the mill is still operated by Rickard descendant Maurice Forte, who comes in on Saturdays and carefully sharpens the millstones and does the grinding. Come sit a spell with him and he will talk your ear off, say volunteers.

In the old days people from miles around gathered at the mill, bringing a "turn" of corn for grinding but, just as importantly, catching up on the latest news in the process. At that time, the grounds also held a blacksmith shop, and syrup was processed here. Today, folks rocking on the Lyin' Porch at the Covered Bridge Gift Shop provide similar entertainment. An old iron bridge has been covered to create the gift shop, which features works by Hand and Eye Folk Pottery artists, other local crafts, books, and gift items.

A cedar swamp is part of the park, and there are several hiking trails, picnic tables, a log cabin, and mules and horses to look at.

Rickard's Mill completes the Swing South Trail; however, if you continue north on State 265, you will come to Camden, where you could extend your trip with the sites on the Black Belt Trail (see details in that chapter).

In a region that gave birth to both the Confederacy and the Civil Rights movement, you'd expect to find many historical attractions and you won't be disappointed. However, we hope you'll also encounter some pleasant surprises too.

Evergreen Chamber of Commerce, 100 Depot Square, Evergreen, AL 36401, 334-578-1707.

Greenville Area Chamber of Commerce, 110 Cedar Street, Greenville, AL 36037, 334-382-3251 or 800-959-0717.

Monroeville Area Chamber of Commerce, P.O. Box 214, Monroeville, AL 36461, 334-743-2879.

Pine Flat Plantation Bed and Breakfast, c/o 1555 Dauphin Street, Mobile, AL 36603, 334-471-8024.

CHAPTER 11

TENNESSEE RIVER HERITAGE TRAIL

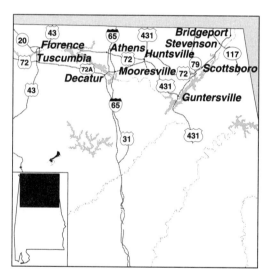

he Cherokees called the mighty river Tenese, a name that was adopted by white pioneers. As it winds its way in a huge crescent across four states from Knoxville, Tennessee to Paducah, Kentucky, the river travels 652 miles, its history mirroring that of the region.

To Native Americans, the river was an essential part of life. To the pioneers, the river was a route to further exploration of the West and an invaluable source of wildlife. To the settlers, the dense forests and fertile bottom lands of the Tennessee Valley were fodder for the emerging nation. In this century the river has been reformed and controlled by modern-day engineers. Visitors come to enjoy the lakes and other attractions created by history and prosperity.

In 1540, the Spanish explorer Hernando De Soto entered the Tennessee Valley in search of the fabled riches of the Aztecs, Mayas, and Incas. Although he found a robust land, he discovered little material wealth.

Initial cordial relations between Native Americans and settlers soon deteriorated into periods of hostility and war. Countless treaties were broken. The river itself became part of the Trail of Tears route used to forcefully move Native Americans from the Southeast to Oklahoma in the 1830s.

During the Civil War, the river often ran red with blood. To the Union, the Tennessee was an artery leading to the heart of the Confederacy. To the Confederacy the river was the primary defense line on the western front. When that line was broken, the stage was set for Sherman's invasion of the Deep South, the fall of Atlanta, and the March to the Sea.

In 1867, a torrential rain caused a flood that not only destroyed many river towns, but also foretold future disasters aggravated by depleted farmland and denuded forests.

After the Civil War the Tennessee River and Valley were largely abandoned as a result of a great western migration. This staggering loss of physical and human assets was not recovered for several generations. So catastrophic were the effects of the Depression on the area that the valley was considered to be the nation's number-one economic problem. Disease and poverty were rampant.

In 1933, President Franklin D. Roosevelt set into motion an unparalleled experiment. The Tennessee Valley Authority (TVA) was created to physically reshape the river and economically transform the surrounding valley. Gigantic dams regulated the water, which was then turned by huge turbines to create abundant, pollution-free electricity while also controlling the periodic flooding and providing jobs to the area. Changing the perilous and unnavigable river into a series of placid lakes was one of the most monumental engineering exploits since the building of the pyramids.

The very best way to explore the Tennessee River—the way well-to-do Southerners might have done in a bygone era—is aboard the authentic New Orleans-based paddlewheeler *Delta Queen* or her newer sisters, *Mississippi Queen* and the *American Queen* (504-586-0631). These are the only two steam-powered paddlewheelers in the country that provide overnight accommodations. On their Wilderness Rivers Cruise, the grande dames of the river call at Florence—former home to both Helen Keller and W. C. Handy—and Decatur, which retains the largest concentration of Victorian homes in Alabama.

If one of the Queens isn't within your budget, your car or RV makes an acceptable substitute. The 197-mile Tennessee River Heritage Driving Tour was created by the TVA and local governments in all three states through which it passes in order to guide travelers through the diverse area. This chapter will explore only the section of the river that flows across northern Alabama. It courses from the extreme northwestern corner of the state through Florence and Muscle Shoals, Wheeler Lake, Decatur, Guntersville, Guntersville Lake, and finally leaves Alabama at its extreme northeastern corner near Bridgeport.

As you travel this route you'll explore attractions relating to prehistoric peoples and pioneers, the Old South and the new South, black heritage, bluegrass, Native American history, and country culture. Opportunities abound for fishing, camping, boating, and hiking.

Begin your tour at the highest point of the Natchez Trace Parkway. This famous 450-mile wilderness trail, laid out in 1802, connected Nashville, Tennessee, and Natchez, Mississippi. The portion in Alabama extends from US 72 north through Colbert and Lauderdale Counties. Abounding in historical and natural sites, the parkway is also the site of Alabama's oldest covered bridge. At Buzzard Roost, a short, paved trail leads down to the spring. A few miles farther along the parkway, signs indicate a steep, quarter-mile trail which leads up to the 800-foot summit of Freedom Mountain Overlook, one of the highest points in Alabama.

At Buzzard Roost Spring on US 72 at the state line, a short trail will lead you to exhibits that relate the story of Levi Colbert, a Chickasaw chief who owned a nearby stand (inn) that served the needs of travelers on the Natchez Trace.

The Tennessee River in Northwest Alabama forms an area known as The Shoals, which includes the Quad Cities of Florence, Muscle Shoals, Sheffield, and Tuscumbia. Information on The Shoals is available from the Colbert County Tourism and Convention Bureau (US 72 West, Tuscumbia; 205-383-0783).

Head east toward Tuscumbia on US 72. At State 247 turn south to visit the Key Underwood Coon Dog Memorial Graveyard. In 1937, Underwood laid his favorite coon dog, Troop, to rest in this spot. Since then, many other faithful companions have been buried here as well (205-383-0783).

Return to US 72 and continue east to **Tuscumbia.** Stop at the Alabama Music Hall of Fame (US 72 West, 800-239-2643), a museum that honors more than five hundred Alabama musicians. Some of those who have contributed to rock and roll, rhythm and blues, gospel, soul, country and western, opera, and classics include Tammy Wynette, Emmylou Harris, the group ALABAMA, The Commodores, Tommy Shaw, W. C. Handy, Hank Williams Jr., and Hank Williams Sr. Just a few of the items on display are Elvis Presley's recording contract; wax figures of Nat King Cole, Hank Williams, and other stars; ALABAMA's tour bus; outfits worn by Lionel Ritchie and the Commodores; and the world's largest guitar—you'll have to see it to believe it. Record your own "hit" in the recording studio and take home your cassette. The Alabama Music Hall of Fame Anniversary Celebration is held each August.

Ivy Green, the birthplace of Helen Keller (300 West North Commons, 205-383-4066), is situated on six hundred and forty acres. The main house was built in 1820 by Helen's grandparents. Helen was born in the cottage adjacent to the main house, in which she later lived with her teacher, Annie Sullivan. The old "whistle path" takes visitors to the outdoor kitchen. Visit the famous water pump in the backyard where the miracle of understanding took place. Among hundreds of personal mementos, of particular interest are Helen's Braille books and Braille typewriter.

Playwright William Gibson's epic drama *The Miracle Worker* is performed on the grounds each year on weekends from late June through late July. Thousands gather in Tuscumbia each June for the annual Helen Keller Festival, a week-long event held to commemorate the town's renowned native.

Admire Colbert County's courthouse. Built in 1881, gutted by fire in 1908, and reconstructed in 1909, it resembles a Victorian wedding cake. The entire district surrounding the courthouse is on the National Register of Historic Districts.

The Ritz Theater (103 West Third Street, 205-383-0533) was built in 1928 during the art-deco period. Beautifully restored, it is the venue for many plays and musical events.

Belle Mont Mansion (US 43 at Cooks Lane, 205-381-5052) is one of Alabama's most distinguished homes. Constructed in the early 1800s, it is an excellent example of Jeffersonian architecture and is known for its high-quality brickwork and contrasting wood trim.

From Tuscumbia, take US 43/State 13 across the river to **Florence.** Named in 1818 for Florence, Italy, the city is embellished with historic buildings and graceful neighborhoods. A brochure for the Historic Florence Walking Tour is available at the Renaissance Tower Visitors Center (One Hightower Place, 205-740-4141).

The Indian Mound at Florence (South Court Street, 205-760-6379), the largest domiciliary mound in the Tennessee Valley, shows the workmanship of early Native Americans. The museum displays historical artifacts that explain Native American culture from the Paleo to Historic periods.

Dedicated to the "Father of the Blues," the W. C. Handy Birthplace and Museum (620 West College Street, 205-760-6434) pays tribute to Handy's extraordinary career. He was born in the small log cabin in 1873 and as a poor youngster took trumpet lessons on a five-dollar trumpet. As one of America's greatest blues composers, Handy gave the world "St. Louis Blues," "Memphis Blues," and "Beale Street Blues." Exhibits include the most complete collection of the famous musician's personal papers and artifacts, his trumpet and the piano on which "St. Louis Blues" was composed, handwritten music, photographs, and a wealth of blues memorabilia. A week-long festival in August celebrates Handy's musical accomplishments.

Pope's Tavern (203 Hermitage Drive, 205-760-6379 or 205-760-6439), one of the oldest structures in Florence, was a stagecoach stop, tavern, and inn and was also used as a hospital by both Confederate and Union troops during the Civil War. In the early nineteenth century, taverns were the center of community life and served as meeting places for business, entertainment, and political activities. This tavern's location on the vital Military Road from Nashville to New Orleans made it an ideal center of commerce. Local legend says that General Andrew Jackson stopped here in 1814 on his way to march into battle against the British in New Orleans.

The tavern is architecturally significant because it represents the southern colonial vernacular style. Today, it serves as a museum featuring pioneer and Civil War artifacts. The annual Frontier Day Celebration the first weekend in June features demonstrations, arts and crafts, storytelling, and dulcimer music.

Soaring above Pickwick Lake, the Renaissance Tower (Union Street and Wilson Dam Highway, Florence, 205-764-5900) is Alabama's tallest tourist attraction. At a height of 300 feet, the tower offers not only a spectacular panorama of the lake and Wilson Lock and Dam, but also houses TVA exhibits, the Alabama Shoals Aquarium with fish from all over the world, and a world-class restaurant. The grounds contain a wildflower garden and nature trail.

Drive by the Rosenbaum House (601 Riverview Drive, 205-764-5274), designed in 1939 by famed architect Frank Lloyd Wright. It is one of the best examples of his Usonian style and the oldest Wright-designed house in the country still occupied by the original owners.

Also in The Shoals area, the Tennessee Valley Art Center (511

North Water Street, Tuscumbia, 205-383-0533) and the Kennedy-Douglass Center for the Arts (217 East Tuscaloosa, Florence, 205-760-6379) present visual exhibitions to the public free of charge. The Kennedy-Douglass Center comprises a Georgian house, a Victorian house, and a carriage house.

Special events in The Shoals area include the Alabama Renaissance Faire held each October at Wilson Park in Florence; Arts Alive, a weekend arts festival in April also held at Wilson Park; and Coldwater Fair held in September in Tuscumbia.

A pleasant place to stay in the Shoals area is Wood Avenue Inn (658 North Wood Avenue, Florence, 205-766-8441), a magnificent 1889 Queen Anne Victorian featuring octagonal and square towers, a generous wrap-around porch, and beautiful gardens.

Take US 72 east to Wheeler Lake. Covering 67,100 acres, Wheeler Lake is the largest of the TVA's three reservoirs in North Alabama. Stretching 60 miles from Wheeler Dam to Guntersville, the lake is ideal for boating, waterskiing, swimming, and trophy fishing. Deep drop-offs and shallow banks, narrow tributaries and wide-open spaces, steep bluffs, rocky points, gravel flats and flooded timbers provide excellent habitats for largemouth, smallmouth, and spotted bass, crappie, channel catfish, and freshwater drum. The best access to the lake is at the Decatur Boat Harbor on US 31.

Wheeler State Park Resort (US 72, Rogersville, 800-544-5639) is part of the Joe Wheeler State Park, which offers 2,550 acres, a lodge, a swimming pool, and a marina as well as a conference center, a restaurant, an eighteen-hole golf course, four lighted, all-weather tennis courts, beaches, and a campground.

Continue on US 72 to **Athens.** Athens–Limestone County is blessed with an abundance of historic homes and sites, many dating back to the early 1800s. For example, the Donnell House (601 Clinton Street, 205-232-0743) was built in 1845 by Cumberland Presbyterian minister Robert Donnell. During the Civil War, the house was commandeered by Union troops. For a short time it served as a public high school, and it is now a living history museum. During the annual April Spring Pilgrimage you can visit many historic homes and churches.

Built in 1842, Athens State College is Alabama's oldest institution of higher learning. Legend says that the college was saved from destruction by Union troops when the College Madam produced a letter written by Abraham Lincoln that presumably asked that the college be spared. Founders Hall (300 North Beaty Street, 205-232-1802) houses the majestic Altar of the New Testament, a life-size tulip-wood carving depicting Christ and New Testament figures and verses. The altar was carved by Eunice McDonald Meadows, a 1913 graduate of the college who carved it while she was artist-in-residence of the college. This masterpiece, which took twelve years to complete, is listed on the National Register of Historic Places.

At the Houston Library and Museum (101 North Houston Street, 205-233-8770) you'll see mementos of George Houston, one of Alabama's most distinguished citizens, who was an attorney, U.S. senator, and two-time governor. The museum features the Houston family coat of arms, portraits, and furniture.

Browns Ferry Energy Connection (Browns Ferry Nuclear Power Plant, 205-729-3300) is a computerized, interactive visitors center where travelers can learn about the TVA. Part of the tour includes an inspection of the nuclear power plant.

From foot-stomping, old-time fiddle music to contemporary tunes, Athens–Limestone County has a special musical event for everyone. Some of Nashville's headliners join local performers to offer the Musical Explosion, a four-day spring family event. Music lovers and musicians from all over the country converge on Athens State College each October for the Tennessee Valley Old Time Fiddlers Convention, which is one of the oldest and largest fiddlers events in the nation. Two days of competition are held in thirteen categories that include harmonica, mandolin, bluegrass, banjo, dulcimer, old-time singing, guitar, and buck dancing. The highlight of the festival is the Fiddle Off between junior and senior fiddle champions dueling for the title of "Fiddle King."

Decatur's Old Bank Building built in 1833

America's rich folk-art history comes alive during the May Home-spun Festival, a two-day arts-and-crafts festival featuring demonstra-tions of pioneer-era skills and live music.

Take US 31 south to **Decatur** in Morgan County, which is the largest cotton producer in the state. In the fall, Morgan County's fields are blanketed in white as if under new-fallen snow. Gigantic pickers snatch up the valuable crop, and other machines compact it into large bales the size of tractor trailers. These bales then stand in the fields like huge powder puffs until they are ready to be shipped.

Although it was founded in the early 1800s as Rhodes Ferry, the city became Decatur in 1823 by order of President James Monroe in honor of the U.S. naval officer Commodore Stephen Decatur. Among his exploits were important naval commands during the War of 1812 and attacks against the Barbary pirates in the Mediterranean. He is best remembered for his toast to "Our country! In her intercourse with foreign nations may she always be in the right; but our country, right or wrong!"

Built in 1833 as one of three branches of the newly created Bank of the State of Alabama, the Decatur facility (925 Bank Street NE, 205-350-5060) was opened in an attempt by President Andrew Jackson to do away with the Bank of the United States. The pre-Greek Revival structure saw an initial period of great success followed by hard times and a banking collapse unprecedented in early Alabama history. It was closed in 1837 and served as a private home until the Civil War. The five limestone columns were pockmarked by Minié balls and musket fire from Union and Confederate troops skirmishing nearby. One column bears the inscription "JKC, Co. A, 12th Regt. Indiana Union." The bank served as a Union hospital during the Civil War and was one of only four buildings left standing in Decatur when the war ended. Today, it houses a museum showcasing Decatur's past. Downstairs the original tellers' cages and safe can be seen. Several years ago, when the Decatur Visitors and Convention Bureau was housed at the bank, employees were forced to take cover in the vaults during a tornado. Upstairs is furniture similar to that which might have been used by the head cashier's family, who lived on the premises.

Farther along Bank Street are revitalized shops from the Victorian era, including an antique mall. The remodeled 1887 Princess Theatre, which first served as a livery stable, was transformed into a theater in 1919 to host high-class road shows, silent movies, and vaudeville acts. A face-lift in 1940 resulted in its present art-deco style. Today, the theater is the site of concerts, ballets, Shakespearean plays, and classic movies.

Decatur claims to have the largest district of Victorian craftsman and bungalow homes in the state. The unique settlement pattern of Decatur resulted in two vibrant districts—the Old Decatur Historic District and the New Albany Historic District. One neighborhood was primarily inhabited by Southerners, the other principally by transplanted Northerners—carpetbaggers. Residents of the two towns didn't mix or date—in fact, they wouldn't even talk to each other. The problem was resolved in 1930 when the two districts were combined into incorporated Decatur.

The Old Decatur Historic District dates from the town's settlement in 1820. Its glamorous homes are primarily from the period between 1870 and 1910, but some were built prior to the Civil War. The town was frequently occupied during that war because of the significance of the Memphis and Charleston Railroad Bridge across the Tennessee River. All but a handful of Decatur's buildings were reduced to ashes by Union troops when the town was evacuated in 1864. Old Decatur is bounded on the west by Bank Street, on the east by Sixth Avenue, on the south by Lee Street, and on the north by Wilson Street.

The New Albany Historic District was so named because many of its first residents in 1887 were wealthy Yankee industrialists from Albany, New York, who brought industry and prosperity back to Decatur. Alternating streets were humorously named after Union and Confederate generals. This neighborhood is bounded on the west by Line Street, on the east by Eleventh Street, on the south by Gordon Street, and on the north by Lee Street. New Albany contains over a hundred late-nineteenth-century homes.

Get the brochure "A Walking Tour of Historic Decatur," which covers both districts, from the Decatur Convention and Visitors Bureau (719 Sixth Avenue SE; 205-350-2028). Driving and Christmas tour brochures are also available.

Cook's Natural Science Museum (412 Thirteenth Street SE, 205-350-9347) exhibits two thousand exotic insects, mounted birds, animals, rocks, minerals, and corals. Rated as one of the top museums in the Southeast, Cook's features touch-and-feel exhibits and—best of all—is free.

Wheeler National Wildlife Refuge (State 67, 205-350-6639), the ultimate bed and breakfast for waterfowl, encompasses 34,500 acres of naturally preserved woodlands on an island created by the Wheeler Dam, a TVA project that backs up the river for seventy-four miles. This refuge offers you a unique opportunity to experience wildlife in its natural habitat. Established in 1938 as an experimental home for waterfowl, the refuge is the natural habitat of Alabama's only concentration of wintering wild geese, the state's largest convergence of ducks, hundreds of deer, and over three hundred species of birds. Givens Wildlife Interpretive Center at the refuge features a glassed-in observation area on Beaverdam Peninsula that looks out on waterfowl nesting grounds. Various displays depict animals common to the region in their natural habitats. Boats, bicycles, and horses are permitted in the refuge, but no ATVs are allowed.

The Racking Horse is the official state horse of Alabama, and the Racking Horse Breeders' Association of America is headquartered in Decatur. The association sponsors two yearly events, the Racking Horse Spring Celebration in April and the Racking Horse World Celebration in September, both held at the Racking Horse Celebration Arena in Priceville (Horse Center Road, 205-353-RACK).

Ever wonder what happens to lost luggage? Some of it comes to the Unclaimed Baggage Center (1836 Sixth Avenue SE, 205-350-0439), a shopper's paradise where you can pick up lots of bargains.

During the year, Decatur sponsors several other outstanding festivals: the Alabama Jubilee Hot Air Balloon Classic held on Memorial Day weekend, the Spirit of America Festival held July 3–4, and the Parade of Boats and Christmas Tour of Homes in December. The Southern Wildlife Festival in November salutes the artistic expression of wildlife with decoy carving, wildlife photography, painting, and duck calling.

In addition to the Holiday Inn, overlooking the river and the Amberly Suites Hotel next door to the Historic Old State Bank, several other chain hotels are available. Indulge yourself with a stay at the historic Dancy-Polk Bed and Breakfast (901 Railroad Street NW, 205-353-3579), an 1829 Palladian-style house, or with a night at the

Hearts and Treasures Bed and Breakfast (911 Seventh Avenue SE, 205-353-9562), a 1920s home.

For a different taste in barbecue, try the white sauce at Big Bob Gibson's Barbecue (1715 Sixth Avenue SE, 205-350-6969). Simp McGhee's (725 Bank Street NE, 205-353-6284) is named after a notorious local character—a turn-of-the-century riverboat captain who had a relationship with a bordello madam and drank beer with his pet pig. Located in a historic building that retains its pressed-tin ceiling and original wooden floor, the restaurant specializes in Cajun dishes.

Take a detour west of Decatur on State 20/Alt. US 72 to the Joe Wheeler Home (12880 State 20, 205-974-1658), the plantation residence of "Fighting" Joe Wheeler (a senior Confederate cavalry leader), his wife, and their seven children. The tree-shaded mansion is fully furnished with Wheeler's personal memorabilia, including items from his service as a U.S. congressman and as a major general in the Spanish-American War.

At age twenty-six, Wheeler was one of the youngest lieutenant generals commissioned in the Army of the Confederate States of America and earned Robert E. Lee's characterization as one of the two outstanding cavalrymen in the War Between the States. (The other was J. E. B. Stuart.) Wheeler's prowess in the Civil War seems all the more amazing when you learn that the lowest grade he received at West Point was in cavalry tactics.

Wheeler's second daughter, Annie, became famous in her own right. During the Spanish-American War, Clara Barton put her in charge of a newly organized hospital in Cuba, where Annie earned the title "Angel of Santiago." She also nursed in a military hospital in the Philippines when her father served there. During World War I, Annie joined the Red Cross and served in England and France. Back at the plantation, she established schools and paved the way for Alabama to offer courses in home economics. Because Annie lived at Wheeler until her death in 1955 and bequeathed the home and its contents to the state, the family artifacts have been preserved. Annie is buried at the rear of the house in the family cemetery.

The three main houses on the plantation are a dogtrot or double log cabin probably built before 1818, a two-story Federal-style house built around the 1820s, and the main Wheeler home built around 1872. Several plantation dependencies also survive.

Return to Decatur and go east on I-565 to Exit 2. Historic **Mooresville,** a tiny community two miles north of Decatur, is older than the state of Alabama. Formed in 1818 before Alabama became a state, the entire twelve blocks of oak-lined streets are listed on the National Register of Historic Places. Young Andrew Johnson worked as a tailor's apprentice here in the 1840s. Local legend holds that during the Civil War future president James A. Garfield took the pulpit at the white frame Church of Christ to read from the Scriptures while his army camped nearby.

In addition to Johnson's home and the Church of Christ, Mooresville boasts an impressive array of early-nineteenth-century structures that are all in private use today. The red-brick community church retains chandeliers and a slave balcony that weathered the Civil War. Few buildings were damaged or destroyed during the war, with the exception of the Female Institute, which was razed. The tavern was the main stagecoach stop from Huntsville to points west. Although it's been an uphill fight to keep it open in compliance with modern post-office regulations, the Mooresville Post Office has been in continuous use since 1844. Wooden cubbyholes that were used to receive mail during the Civil War are still used by residents today.

"A Walking Tour of Mooresville" brochure can be purchased at the Post Office. Homes are open for tours every other year.

While in the vicinity of Mooresville, treat yourself to a scrumptious catfish or barbecue meal at the well-known Greenbrier Restaurant (27028 Old State 20, 205-351-1800) which is not to be confused with Greenbrier Bar-B-Q. Located two miles along Greenbrier Road off I-565 near Mooresville, the family restaurant began in a one-room structure in 1952. Although it has been enlarged numerous times, the restaurant retains its simple ambience.

Special events in Morgan County include Somerville's June Wagon Train, down-home fun with camping, bonfires, and story-

telling; Eva Frontier Days held each September, a week-long celebration that includes a parade, a crafts show, a barbecue, and old-
fashioned demonstrations; Hartselle's Depot Days held Labor Day
weekend with a street dance, a picnic, a talent show, and a car show;
and Morgan City's Founders Day held the first weekend in June with
a parade, an Old West shootout, arts and crafts, clogging, an antique-
car show, and a pancake breakfast. Tours of homes are held in April
in Decatur and Hartselle, and in December in Florence and Decatur.

From Decatur take I-565 northeast to **Huntsville.** Called the Sil-
icon Valley of the South, Huntsville is one of the fastest-growing
cities in the nation and is now best known for the Space and Rocket
Center (1 Tranquility Base, 205-837-3400), the world's largest space
museum. The city had a sleepy beginning—from its infancy as a single log cabin built by John Hunt in 1805, Huntsville became the first
English-speaking settlement in Alabama. The town developed into a
transportation hub where river barges, stagecoach lines, and railroads
converged. Once the temporary capital of Alabama, it was occupied
by Federal troops during the Civil War, and luckily only a few structures were destroyed.

Early in this century, tourism was encouraged with the develop-
ment of Monte Sano Mountain as a vacation health resort. Then
World War II changed everything. Two major arsenals became the
Redstone Arsenal. Space research and development poured in after
Wernher von Braun and his elite team of rocket scientists migrated
to Redstone, which became the center for all U.S. rocket research.

Don't neglect the past while you're in Huntsville. Two neighborhoods that are on the National Register of Historic Places—Twick-
enham and Old Town—offer a four-mile living museum of eighteen
decades of architecture.

Alabama's Constitution Village (404 Madison Street, 205-535-
6565 or 800-678-1819), the meeting place of Alabama's 1819 Con-
stitutional Convention, is a living-history village where costumed
guides and craftspeople depict life in Alabama from 1805 to 1819.

The Huntsville Depot Museum (320 Church Street, 205-539-
1860 or 800-239-8955) is Alabama's oldest surviving railroad depot

and one of the oldest depots in the country. In addition to a multi-media presentation on the history of Huntsville and its depot, you'll find a trolley, rolling stock, a working turntable, a roundhouse, a 1/8-scale narrow-gauge steam locomotive, an HO-scale model railroad, that recreates Huntsville as it was in the 1860s, and Andy Barker, the robotic ticket agent and telegrapher who operates a 1912 telegraph office.

The 1900 Harrison Brothers Hardware Store (124 South Side Square, 205-536-3631) is Alabama's oldest hardware store. Built in 1897, it has been in continuous operation ever since.

Despite Huntsville's historical significance, the city is perhaps best known for its technological achievements. Launch into space adventure at the U.S. Space and Rocket Center/NASA Visitor Center (Tranquility Base, 205-837-3400 or 800-63-SPACE), the world's largest space science museum. Its many displays fire the imaginations of visitors regardless of their ages.

If you remain overnight in Huntsville, stay at the Stockton House Bed and Breakfast Inn (310 Green Street SE, 205-539-3195), a graceful 1910 Queen Anne Victorian house.

Another choice is Wandlers Inn (101 Shawnee Drive NW, 205-837-6694), a bed and breakfast where a one-bedroom apartment is located in a restored antebellum barn and is rented on a nightly basis.

Take a short trip east on US 72 to **Chase** to visit the North Alabama Railroad Museum (694 Chase Road, 205-881-3629). In the waiting room and agent's office of the small Chase Depot are displays depicting railroad history in northern Alabama. More than twenty-five passenger and freight cars and two locomotives have been preserved. The museum sponsors annual excursions from Huntsville to Chattanooga.

Return to Huntsville and go southeast on US 431/State 1 to **Guntersville.** At the Lake Guntersville Aero Replica Fighter Museum (US 431/State 1 North, 205-582-3612) you'll see the world's largest collection of original and replica World War I aircraft, full-scale and model planes, antique automobiles, and nose art (decorations on the nose of a plane). You can also watch skilled craftsmen restoring planes to their original glory. Check for the museum's schedule of simulated dogfights and flybys.

Lake Guntersville itself is thirty miles long. The Lake Guntersville State Park (1155 Lodge Drive, 205-582-3612) sits high atop a 500-foot bluff overlooking the lake and offers a pool, fishing, boating, waterskiing, hiking, tennis, and golf. The lodge is nestled on Little Mountain and affords sweeping views of the river. Accommodations are also offered in cottages and at primitive and improved campsites.

Retrace US 431/State 1 north to State 79 and proceed northeast. When you get to US 72, turn right toward **Scottsboro,** which is known for its First Monday Trade Day. The vibrant and active downtown square of Scottsboro is perfect for window-shopping and antiquing. Payne's Cafe is popular with locals and visitors partly because of its old-fashioned soda fountain.

The Heritage Center is located just east of the square in the 1880s Brown-Proctor mansion (208 South Houston Street, 205-259-2122). Fascinating displays and photographs trace rural life before TVA electrification. Behind the mansion is Sagetown, a pioneer village created by moving authentic structures to the site. Explore the tiny original Jackson County Courthouse as well as a pioneer cabin, a barn, a blacksmith shop, a schoolhouse, and a mine.

Five miles south of Scottsboro off State 279 is Goose Pond Colony Park (205-582-3612). Rental cottages and campgrounds dot the shoreline of the lake. Championship golf and fishing compete for your attention. Other facilities include a pool, an amphitheater, a scenic walking trail, a marina, and a bait and tackle shop.

Continue north on US 72 and head northwest on State 117 to **Stevenson.** Stevenson was one of seven important railroad junctions in the South during the Civil War. The restored 1850s Stevenson Depot Museum (Main Street, 205-437-3012) evokes memories of the area's past through exhibits on Indian heritage and railroading history, Civil War artifacts, and farm tools.

Return to US 72 and go north to **Bridgeport,** named for a railroad bridge that was a major supply route during the Civil War. Still operating after a hundred and thirty years, the Reese's Heritage Ferry (259-5500) at Bridgeport is the only ferry in Alabama that crosses the Tennessee River and one of only three ferries in the entire state. The free trip across the river gives you an unusual vista of the river and its surroundings.

From US 72 turn west on County 91, then northwest on County 75 to Russell Cave National Monument (3729 County 98, 205-495-2672). Although it is now known that the cave was used as a natural shelter 9,000 years ago, no relics were discovered until 1953. In addition to a tour of the cave, the park features a visitors center, hiking and horseback trails, and an Indian Garden. Skilled park rangers demonstrate ancient arts such as tool cutting, arrowhead-making, and spear throwing.

The Tennessee River leaves Alabama and flows into Tennessee just north of Bridgeport.

For several hundred years the Tennessee River provided water, food, and transportation for Native Americans and early settlers. Today, in addition to transportation and hydro-elctric power, the river offers countless recreational activities, making it an ideal vacation destination.

Alabama Welcome Center (I-59 south of Georgia state line), P.O. Box 846, Collinsville, AL 35961, 205-635-6522.

Ardmore Welcome Center (I-65 south of Tennessee state line), 26865 I-65, Elkmont, AL 35620, 205-423-3891.

Athens/Limestone County Chamber of Commerce, 101 Beaty Street, Athens, AL 35611, 205-232-2600.

Chamber of Commerce of The Shoals, 104 South Pine Street, Florence, AL 35630, 205-764-4661.

Colbert County Tourism and Convention Bureau, State 72 West, Tuscumbia, AL 35674, 205-383-0783.

Decatur Convention and Visitors Bureau, 719 Sixth Avenue SE, Decatur, AL 35601, 205-350-2028.

Delta Queen Steamship Company, 30 Robin Street Wharf, New Orleans, LA 70130-1890, 504-586-0631.

Lake Guntersville Chamber of Commerce, 200 Gunter Avenue, Guntersville, AL 35976, 205-582-3612.

Marshall County Tourism Commission, 200 Gunter Avenue, Guntersville, AL 35976, 205-582-7015.

Huntsville–Madison County Convention and Visitors Bureau, 700 Monroe Street, Huntsville, AL 35801, 205-551-2230.

Scottsboro–Jackson County Chamber of Commerce, 407 East Willow Street, Scottsboro, AL 35768, 205-259-5500.

CHAPTER 12

HELPFUL
CONTACTS

Alabama Bureau of Tourism and Travel
401 Adams Avenue
Montgomery, AL 36103-4309
phone: 334-242-4169 or 800-ALABAMA
fax: 334-242-4554

Alabama Travel Council
702 Oliver Road
Montgomery, AL 36117
phone: 334-271-0050
fax: 334-279-7798

AAA Alabama Motorists Association
State Headquarters
2305 Fifth Avenue North
Birmingham, AL 35203
phone: 205-323-4491

Alabama Mountain Lakes Association
25062 North Street
Mooresville, AL 35649-1075
phone: 205-350-3500 or 800-648-5381
fax: 205-350-3519

The Black Belt Tourism Council
P.O. Drawer D
Selma, AL 36702
phone: 334-875-7241

Historic Chattahoochee Commission
211 North Eufaula Avenue
Eufaula, AL 36027
phone: 334-687-9755
fax: 334-687-6631

INDEX

COUNTRY ROADS PRESS

Country Roads Press publishes books that celebrate the spirit and flavor of rural and small town America. Far from strip malls and chain stores, the heart of America may still be found among the people and in the places along its country roads. Country Roads Press invites its readers to travel those roads with us.

Titles in the Country Roads series:

Country Roads of Alabama $10.95
Country Roads of Connecticut and Rhode Island
Country Roads of Florida
Country Roads of Georgia
Country Roads of Hawaii
Country Roads of Idaho
Country Roads of Illinois, second edition
Country Roads of Indiana
Country Roads of Iowa
Country Roads of Kentucky
Country Roads of Louisiana $10.95
Country Roads of Maine
Country Roads of Maritimes
Country Roads of Maryland and Delaware
Country Roads of Massachusetts
Country Roads of Michigan, second edition
Country Roads of Minnesota
Country Roads of Missouri
Country Roads of New Hampshire, second edition
Country Roads of New Jersey, second edition $10.95
Country Roads of New York
Country Days in New York City
Country Roads of North Carolina
Country Roads of Ohio, second edition $10.95
Country Roads of Ontario
Country Roads of Oregon
Country Roads of Pennsylvania
Country Roads of Southern California
Country Roads of Tennessee
Country Roads of Texas
Country Roads of Vermont
Country Roads of Virginia
Country Roads of Washington
Country Roads of Wisconsin $10.95

All other prices, $9.95. All books are available at bookstores. Prices subject to change. Or order directly from the publisher (add $3.00 shipping & handling for direct orders):

Country Roads Press
P.O. Box 838
Oaks, Pennsylvania 19456
(610) 666-9763